A Brief Introduction to Jainism and Sikhism

A Brief Introduction to
JAINISM AND SIKHISM

Updated and revised by Tim Dowley

General Editor: Christopher Partridge

Fortress Press

Minneapolis

A BRIEF INTRODUCTION TO JAINISM AND SIKHISM

The maps and images on pages 120-121 appear in *Atlas of World Religions*
(Fortress Press, forthcoming).

Cover image: Mahavira y Tirtankaras/Seattle Asian Art Museum/© Miguel Hermoso
Cuesta/Wikimedia Commons; Golden Temple, Holiest shrine of the Sikh religion/
JeremyRichard/Shutterstock.com
Cover design: Laurie Ingram

Print ISBN: 978-1-5064-5038-4
eBook ISBN: 978-1-5064-5039-1

The paper used in this publication meets the minimum requirements of American
National Standard for Information Sciences — Permanence of Paper for Printed
Library Materials, ANSI Z329.48-1984.

Manufactured in the USA

Contents

PART 1
UNDERSTANDING RELIGION

PART 2
JAINISM

PART 3
SIKHISM

Contributors

Resham Singh Bhogal: *I am a Sikh*

Dr Fiona Bowie, Honorary Research Fellow, Department of Archaeology and Anthropology, University of Bristol, UK: *The Anthropology of Religion, Ritual and Performance*

Dr Jeremy Carrette, Professor of Religion and Culture, University of Kent, England: *Critical Theory and Religion*

Dr Douglas Davies, Professor in the Study of Religion, Department of Theology and Religion, University of Durham, UK: *Myths and Symbols, The Golden Temple*

Dr Malcolm Hamilton, Senior Lecturer, Department of Sociology, University of Reading, UK: *The Sociology of Religion*

Dr Elizabeth J. Harris, Senior Lecturer, Comparative Study of Religions, Liverpool Hope University, UK: *Buddhism: Beliefs, Family and Society, Buddhism in the Modern World*

Dr Paul Hedges, Senior Lecturer in Theology and Religious Studies: *Theological Approaches to the Study of Religion*

Dr Sewa Singh Kalsi, Lecturer in Sikh Studies, University of Leeds, UK: *Sikhism: Sacred Writings, Beliefs, Worship and Festivals, Family and Society*

Magdalen Lambkin, PhD, University of Glasgow, Scotland: Consultant, *Understanding Religion*

Dr Russell T. McCutcheon, Professor of Sociology of Religion, University of Alabama, USA: *What is Religion?*

Dr Christopher Partridge, Professor of Religious Studies, University of Lancaster, UK: *Phenomenology and the Study of Religion, Rapid Fact-finder*

Samani Charitra Prajna: *I am a Jain*

Dr Emma Salter, Course leader, Religion and Education, University of Huddersfield, UK: *Jainism: A Historical Overview, Sacred Writings, Beliefs, Family and Society, Worship and Festivals, Jainism in the Modern World*

Dr Christopher Shackle, Emeritus Professor of Modern Languages of South Asia, University of London, UK: *Sikhism: A Historical Overview, Sikhism Today*

Revd Angela Tilby, Diocesan Canon, Christ Church, Oxford, UK: *Rapid Fact-finder*

Dr Fraser N. Watts, Starbridge Lecturer in Theology and Natural Science, University of Cambridge, UK: *The Psychology of Religion*

Dr Paul Williams, Emeritus Professor of Indian and Tibetan Philosophy, University of Bristol, UK: *Buddhism: A Historical Overview, Sacred Writings*

Revd Dr John-David Yule, Incumbent of the United Benefice of Fen Drayton with Conington, Lolworth, and Swavesey, Cambridge, UK: *Rapid Fact-finder*

List of Maps

List of Time Charts

List of Festival Charts

List of Illustrations

Preface

This volume and five other titles in the *Brief Introductions* series are taken directly from the third edition of *Introduction to World Religions*, edited by Christopher Partridge and revised by Tim Dowley. Additional maps and images are included from *Atlas of World Religions*, edited by Tim Dowley. We recognized that smaller volumes focused on specific religious traditions might be especially helpful for use in corresponding religious studies courses. General readers who are eager to know and understand more about religious beliefs and practices will find this series to be an engaging and accessible way to explore the world's religions—one by one.

Other Books in the Series

A Brief Introduction to Buddhism
A Brief Introduction to Christianity
A Brief Introduction to Hinduism
A Brief Introduction to Islam
A Brief Introduction to Judaism

PART I
UNDERSTANDING RELIGION

SUMMARY

Belief in something that exists beyond or outside our understanding – whether spirits, gods, or simply a particular order to the world – has been present at every stage in the development of human society, and has been a major factor in shaping much of that development. Unsurprisingly, many have devoted themselves to the study of religion, whether to understand a particular set of beliefs, or to explain why humans seem instinctively drawn to religion. While biologists, for example, may seek to understand what purpose religion served in our evolutionary descent, we are concerned here with the beliefs, rituals, and speculation about existence that we – with some reservation – call religion.

The question of what 'religion' actually is is more fraught than might be expected. Problems can arise when we try to define the boundaries between religion and philosophy when speculation about existence is involved, or between religion and politics when moral teaching or social structure are at issue. In particular, once we depart from looking at the traditions of the West, many contend that such apparently obvious distinctions should not be applied automatically.

While there have always been people interested in the religious traditions of others, such 'comparative' approaches are surprisingly new. Theology faculties are among the oldest in European universities, but, while the systematic internal exploration of a religion provides considerable insights, many scholars insisted that the examination of religions more generally should be conducted instead by objective observers. This phenomenological approach was central to the establishment of the study of religion as a discipline in its own right. Others, concerned with the nature of society, or the workings of the human mind, for example, were inevitably drawn to the study of religion to expand their respective areas. More recently, many have attempted to utilise the work of these disparate approaches. In particular, many now suggest that – because no student can ever be entirely objective – theological studies are valuable because of their ability to define a religion in its own terms: by engaging with this alongside other, more detached, approaches, a student may gain a more accurate view of a particular religion.

CHAPTER I

What Is Religion?

Although no one is certain of the word's origins, we know that 'religion' derives from Latin, and that languages influenced by Latin have equivalents to the English word 'religion'. In Germany, the systematic study of religion is known as *Religionswissenschaft*, and in France as *les sciences religieuses*. Although the ancient words to which we trace 'religion' have nothing to do with today's meanings — it may have come from the Latin word that meant to tie something tightly (*religare*) — it is today commonly used to refer to those beliefs, behaviours, and social institutions which have something to do with speculations on any, and all, of the following: the origin, end, and significance of the universe; what happens after death; the existence and wishes of powerful, non-human beings such as spirits, ancestors, angels, demons, and gods; and the manner in which all of this shapes human behaviour.

Because each of these makes reference to an invisible (that is, non-empirical) world that somehow lies outside of, or beyond, human history, the things we name as 'religious' are commonly thought to be opposed to those institutions which we label as 'political'. In the West today we generally operate under the assumption that, whereas religion is a matter of personal belief that can never be settled by rational debate, such things as politics are observable, public, and thus open to rational debate.

THE ESSENCE OF 'RELIGION'

Although this commonsense distinction between private and public, sentiment and action, is itself a historical development — it is around the seventeenth century that we first see evidence that words that once referred to one's behaviour, public standing, and social rank (such as piety and reverence) became sentimentalized as matters of private feeling — today the assumption that religion involves an inner core of belief that is somehow expressed publicly in ritual is so widespread that to question it appears counterintuitive. It is just this assumption that inspires a number of people who, collectively, we could term 'essentialists'. They are 'essentialists' because they maintain that 'religion' names the outward behaviours that are inspired by the inner thing they call 'faith'. Hence, one can imagine someone saying, 'I'm not religious, but I'm spiritual.' Implicit here is the assumption that the institutions associated with religions — hierarchies, regulations, rituals, and so on — are merely secondary and inessential; the important thing is the inner faith, the inner 'essence' of religion. Although the essence of religion – the thing without which someone is thought to be non-religious – is known by various names (faith, belief, the Sacred, the Holy, and so on), essentialists are in general agreement that the essence of religion is real and non-empirical (that is, it cannot itself be seen, heard, touched, and so on); it defies study and must be experienced first-hand.

THE FUNCTION OF 'RELIGION'

Apart from an approach that assumes an inner experience, which underlies religious behaviour, scholars have used the term 'religion' for what they consider to be curious areas of observable human behaviour which require an explanation. Such people form theories to account for why it is people think, for example, that an invisible part of their body, usually called 'the soul', outlives that body; that powerful beings control the universe; and that there is more to existence than what is observable. These theories are largely functionalist; that is, they seek to determine the social, psychological, or political role played by the things we refer to as 'religious'. Such functionalists include historically:

- Karl Marx (1818–83), whose work in political economy understood religion to be a pacifier that deadened oppressed people's sense of pain and alienation, while simultaneously preventing them from doing something about their lot in life, since ultimate responsibility was thought to reside in a being who existed outside history.

Karl Marx (1818–83).

- Émile Durkheim (1858–1917), whose sociology defined religious as sets of beliefs and practices to enable individuals who engaged in them to form a shared, social identity.
- Sigmund Freud (1856–1939), whose psychological studies prompted him to liken religious behaviour to the role that dreams play in helping people to vent antisocial anxieties in a manner that does not threaten their place within the group.

Although these classic approaches are all rather different, each can be understood as *functionalist* insomuch as religion names an institution that has a role to play in helping individuals and communities to reproduce themselves.

THE FAMILY RESEMBLANCE APPROACH

Apart from the *essentialist* way of defining religion (i.e. there is some non-empirical, core feature without which something is not religious) and the *functionalist* (i.e. that religions help to satisfy human needs), there is a third approach: the *family resemblance* definition. Associated with the philosophy of Ludwig Wittgenstein (1889–1951), a family resemblance approach assumes that nothing is defined by merely one essence or function. Rather, just as members of a family more or less share a series of traits, and just as all things we call 'games' more or less share a series of traits – none of which is distributed evenly across all members of those groups we call 'family' or 'games' – so all things – including religion – are defined insomuch as they more or less share a series of delimited traits. Ninian Smart (1927–2001), who identified seven dimensions of religion that are present in religious traditions with varying degrees of emphasis, is perhaps the best known proponent of this view.

'RELIGION' AS CLASSIFIER

Our conclusion is that the word 'religion' likely tells us more about the user of the word (i.e. the classifier) than it does about the thing being classified. For instance, a Freudian psychologist will not conclude that religion functions to oppress the masses, since the Freudian theory precludes coming up with this Marxist conclusion. On the other hand, a scholar who adopts Wittgenstein's approach will sooner or later come up with a case in which something seems to share some traits, but perhaps not enough to count as 'a religion'. If, say, soccer matches satisfy many of the criteria of a religion, what might not also be called religion if soccer is? And what does such a broad usage do to the specificity, and thus utility, of the word 'religion'? As for those who adopt an essentialist approach, it is likely no coincidence that only those institutions with which one agrees are thought to be expressions of some authentic inner experience, sentiment, or emotion, whilst the traditions of others are criticized as being shallow and derivative.

So what is religion? As with any other item in our lexicon, 'religion' is a historical artefact that different social actors use for different purposes: to classify certain parts of their social world in order to celebrate, degrade, or theorize about them. Whatever else it may or may not be, religion is at least an item of rhetoric that group members use to sort out their group identities.

RUSSELL T. MCCUTCHEON

CHAPTER 2

Phenomenology and the Study of Religion

There is a long history of curiosity and scholarship regarding the religions of other people. However, the study of religions is a relative newcomer to academia. Greatly indebted to the impressive work and influence of the German scholar Friedrich Max Müller (1823–1900), the first university professorships were established in the final quarter of the nineteenth century. By the second half of the twentieth century, the study of religion had emerged as an important field of academic enquiry. In a period of history during which the rationalism of the earlier part of the century saw a decline, and in which there was increased interest in particularly non-Christian spirituality, since 1945 there has been a growth in courses in the study of religion offered in academic institutions. Moreover, work done in other disciplines has increasingly converged with the work done by students of religion (see the discussion in this book of 'The Anthropology of Religion', 'The Psychology of Religion', 'The Sociology of Religion', and 'Critical Theory and Religion').

These factors, amongst others, have made it possible for the study of religion in most Western universities to pull away from its traditional place alongside the study of Christian theology and establish itself as an independent field of enquiry. Whereas earlier in the century the study of non-Christian faiths was usually undertaken in faculties of Christian theology, and studied as part of a theology degree, there was a move – particularly in the late 1960s and 1970s, when the term 'religious studies' became common currency – to establish separate departments of religious studies. Whilst in the United States and most of Western Europe religious studies tends to be considered a subject completely distinct from theology, in the United Kingdom it is quite common for universities to offer degree programmes in 'theology and religious studies', and the lines between the two disciplines are not so heavily drawn.

RELIGIONSPHÄNOMENOLOGIE

Phenomenology is distinct from other approaches to the study of religion in that it does not necessarily seek to understand the social nature of religion, it is not concerned to explore the psychological factors involved in religious belief, nor is it

especially interested in the historical development of religions. Rather its main concern has been descriptive, the classification of religious phenomena: objects, rituals, teachings, behaviours, and so on.

During the Kumbh Mela festival in the holy city of Haridwar the Guru in his decorated chariot is escorted by holy men and pilgrims visiting the River Ganges, India.

The term *Religionsphänomenologie* was first used by the Dutch scholar Pierre Daniel Chantepie de la Saussaye (1848–1920) in his work *Lehrbuch der Religions-geschichte* (1887), which simply documented religious phenomena. This might be described as 'descriptive' phenomenology, the aim being to gather information about the various religions and, as botanists might classify plants, identify varieties of particular religious phenomena. This classification of types of religious phenomena, the hallmark of the phenomenological method, can be seen in the works of scholars such as Ninian Smart (1927–2001) and Mircea Eliade (1907–86). Descriptive phenomenology of the late nineteenth and early twentieth centuries tended to lead to accounts of religious phenomena which, to continue with the analogy, read much the same as a botanical handbook. Various species were identified (higher religion, lower religion, prophetic religion, mystical religion, and so on) and particular religious beliefs and practices were then categorized, discussed, and compared.

As the study of religion progressed, phenomenology came to refer to a method which was more complex, and claimed rather more for itself, than Chantepie's mere

A BRIEF INTRODUCTION TO JAINISM AND SIKHISM

cataloguing of facts. This later development in the discipline – which was due in part to the inspiration of the philosophy of Edmund Husserl (1859–1938) – recognized how easy it is for prior beliefs and interpretations unconsciously to influence one's thinking. Hence, scholars such as Gerardus van der Leeuw (1890–1950) stressed the need for phenomenological *epoché*: the 'bracketing' or shelving of the question about the ontological or objective status of the religious appearances to consciousness. Thus questions about the objective or independent truth of Kali, Allah, or the Holy Spirit are initially laid aside. The scholar seeks to suspend judgment about the beliefs of those he studies in order to gain greater objectivity and accuracy in understanding. Also central to phenomenology is the need for empathy (*Einfühlung*), which helps towards an understanding of the religion from within. Students of a religion seek to feel their way into the beliefs of others by empathizing with them. Along with this suspension of judgment and empathy, phenomenologists spoke of 'eidetic vision', the capacity of the observer to see beyond the particularities of a religion and to grasp its core essence and meaning. Whilst we often see only what we want, or expect, to see, eidetic vision is the ability to see a phenomenon without such distortions and limitations. Hence, later phenomenologists did not merely catalogue the facts of religious history, but by means of *epoché*, empathy, and eidetic vision sought to understand their meaning for the believer. Although phenomenologists are well aware that there will always be some distance between the believer's understandings of religious facts and those of the scholar, the aim of phenomenology is, as far as possible, to testify only to what has been observed. It aims to strip away all that would stand in the way of a neutral, judgment-free presentation of the facts.

THE IDEA OF THE HOLY

Some scholars have gone beyond this simple presentation of the facts and claimed more. A classic example is Rudolf Otto's (1869–1937) book *Das Heilige* (*The Idea of the Holy*, 1917). On the basis of his study of religions, Otto claimed that central to all religious expression is an a priori sense of 'the numinous' or 'the holy'. This, of course, necessarily goes beyond a simple presentation of the facts of religious history to the development of a particular philosophical interpretation of those facts. The central truth of all religion, claimed Otto, is a genuine feeling of awe or reverence in the believer, a sense of the 'uncanny' inspired by an encounter with the divine. Otto did more than simply relate facts about religion; he assumed the existence of the holy – accepting the truth of encounters with the supernatural.

> 'Numinous dread' or awe characterizes the so-called 'religion of primitive man', where it appears as 'daemonic dread.'
>
> Rudolf Otto, *The Idea of the Holy*

For some scholars, for example Ninian Smart, such an assumption is unacceptable in the study of religion. To compromise objectivity in this way, Smart argued, skews the scholar's research and findings. What the scholar ends up with is not an unbiased account of the facts of religion, but a personal *theology* of religion.

NEUTRALITY

Whilst Otto's type of phenomenology clearly displays a basic lack of objectivity, it is now generally recognized that this is a problem intrinsic to the study of religions. Although many contemporary religious studies scholars would want to defend the notion of *epoché* as an ideal to which one should aspire, there is a question as to whether this ideal involves a certain naivety. For example, the very process of selection and production of typologies assumes a level of interpretation. To select certain facts rather than others, and to present them with other facts as a particular type of religion, presupposes some interpretation. What facts we consider important and unimportant, interesting or uninteresting, will be shaped by certain ideas that we hold, whether religious or non-religious. To be an atheist does not in itself make the scholar more objective and neutral. Hence, the belief in detached objectivity, and the claim to be purely 'descriptive', are now considered to be naive. The important thing is that, as we engage in study, we recognize and critically evaluate our beliefs, our presuppositions, our biases, and how they might shape the way we understand a religion (see 'Critical Theory and Religion').

INSIDERS AND OUTSIDERS

Another important issue in contemporary religious studies is the 'insider/outsider' problem. To what extent can a non-believer ('an outsider') understand a faith in the way the believer (an 'insider') does? It is argued that outsiders, simply because they are outsiders, will never fully grasp the insider's experience; even people who experience the same event at the same time will, because of their contexts and personal histories, interpret that experience in different ways. However, some scholars have insisted there is a definite advantage to studying religion from the outside – sometimes referred to as the 'etic' perspective. Members of a religion may be conditioned by, or pressurized into accepting, a particular – and often narrow – understanding of their faith, whereas the outsider is in the scholarly position of not being influenced by such pressures and conditioning. Impartiality and disinterest allow greater objectivity.

There is undoubtedly value in scholarly detachment. However – while the scholar may have a greater knowledge of the history, texts, philosophy, structure, and social implications of a particular faith than the average believer – not to have experienced that faith from the inside is surely to have a rather large hole in the centre of one's understanding. Indeed, many insiders will insist that scholarly 'head-knowledge' is peripheral to the 'meaning' of their faith. Hence, others have noted the value of studying a religion as an 'insider', or at least relying heavily on the views of insiders – sometimes referred to as the 'emic' perspective.

RESPONSE THRESHOLD

In order to take account of the emic perspective, along with the emphasis on participant observation (see 'The Anthropology of Religion'), some have spoken of the 'response threshold' in religious studies. The crossing of the response threshold happens when insiders question the scholar's interpretations: etic interpretations are challenged by emic perspectives. An insider's perspective – which may conflict with scholarly interpretations – is felt to carry equal, if not more, weight. Wilfred Cantwell Smith (1916–2000) has even argued that no understanding of a faith is valid until it has been acknowledged by an insider. Religious studies are thus carried out in the context of a dialogue which takes seriously the views of the insider, in order to gain a deeper understanding of the insider's world view.

BEYOND PHENOMENOLOGY

In his book entitled *Beyond Phenomenology* (1999), Gavin Flood has argued that what is important in studying religions is 'not so much the distinction between the insider and the outsider, but between the critical and the non-critical'. Flood makes use of theories developed within the social sciences and humanities. With reference to the shift in contemporary theoretical discourse, which recognizes that all knowledge is tradition-specific and embodied within particular cultures (see 'Critical Theory and Religion'), Flood argues, firstly, that religions should not be abstracted and studied apart from the historical, political, cultural, linguistic, and social contexts. Secondly, he argues that scholars, who are likewise shaped by their own contexts, always bring conceptual baggage to the study of religion. Hence, whether because of the effect research has on the community being studied, or because the scholar's own prejudices, preconceptions, instincts, emotions, and personal characteristics significantly influence that research, the academic study of religion can never be neutral and purely objective. Flood thus argues for 'a rigorous metatheoretical discourse' in religious studies. Metatheory is the critical analysis of theory and practice, the aim of which is to 'unravel the underlying assumptions inherent in any research programme and to critically comment on them'.

Metatheory is thus important because it 'questions the contexts of inquiry, the nature of inquiry, and the kinds of interests represented in inquiry'. In so doing, it questions the idea of detached objectivity in the study of religion, and the notion that one can be a disinterested observer who is able to produce neutral descriptions of religious phenomena, free of evaluative judgments. Hence, scholars need always to engage critically with, and take account of, their own assumptions, prejudices, and presuppositions.

This means that holding a particular faith need not be a hindrance to the study of religion. One can, for example, be a Christian theologian and a good student of religion. But for scholars such as Flood, the important thing is not the faith or lack of it, but the awareness of, and the critical engagement with, one's assumptions: 'It is critique rather than faith that is all important.'

It is worth noting that recent work, mainly in France, sees new possibilities for the philosophy of religion through a turn to phenomenology. Much of this work has been done in response to the important French Jewish philosopher Emmanuel Levinas (1905–95). The names particularly associated with this turn are Jean-Luc Marion, Dominique Janicaud, Jean-Luc Chretien, Michel Henry, and Alain Badiou. Marion, for example, has written on the phenomenology of the gift in theology, Badiou has responded to Levinas arguing against his emphasis on the importance of 'the other', and Chretien has written on the phenomenology of prayer.

CHRISTOPHER PARTRIDGE

CHAPTER 3

The Anthropology of Religion

Anthropology approaches religion as an aspect of culture. Religious beliefs and practices are important because they are central to the ways in which we organize our social lives. They shape our understanding of our place in the world, and determine how we relate to one another and to the rest of the natural, and supernatural, order. The truth or falsity of religious beliefs, or the authenticity or moral worth of religious practices, are seldom an issue for anthropologists, whose main concern is to document what people think and do, rather than determine what they ought to believe, or how they should behave.

RELIGION AND SOCIAL STRUCTURE

An early observation in the anthropology of religion was the extent to which religion and social structure mirror one another. Both the French historian Fustel de Coulanges (1830–89), drawing on Classical sources, and the Scottish biblical scholar William Robertson Smith (1846–94), who studied Semitic religions, demonstrated this coincidence in form. For example, nomadic peoples such as the Bedouin conceive of God in terms

> *The belief in a supreme God or a single God is no mere philosophical speculation; it is a great practical idea.*
>
> Maurice Hocart

of a father, and use familial and pastoral imagery to describe their relationship with God. A settled, hierarchical society, by contrast, will depict God as a monarch to whom tribute is due, with imagery of servants and subjects honouring a supreme ruler. These early studies influenced the French sociologist Émile Durkheim (1858–1917), whose book *The Elementary Forms of the Religious Life* (1912) was foundational for later anthropological studies of religion. Rather than seeing religion as determining social structure, Durkheim argued that religion is a projection of society's highest values and goals. The realm of the sacred is separated from the profane world and made to seem both natural and obligatory. Through collective rituals people both reaffirm their belief in supernatural beings and reinforce their bonds with one another.

The totemism of Australian Aboriginals, which links human groups with particular forms of animal or other natural phenomena in relations of prohibition and prescription, was regarded by many nineteenth-century scholars as the earliest form of religion, and as such was of interest to both Durkheim and the anthropologist Edward Burnett Tylor

(1832–1917), who postulated an evolutionary movement from animism to polytheism and then monotheism. However, as evolutionary arguments are essentially unprovable, later work built not on these foundations, but on the more sociological insights of Durkheim and anthropologists such as Alfred Radcliffe-Brown (1881–1955) and Sir Edward Evan Evans-Pritchard (1902–73).

Evans-Pritchard sought to retain the historical perspective of his predecessors, while replacing speculation concerning origins with data based on first-hand observations and participation in the life of a people. His classic 1937 ethnography of witchcraft, oracles, and magic among the Azande in Central Africa demonstrated that beliefs which, from a Western perspective, appear irrational and unscientific – such as the existence of witches and magic – are perfectly logical, once one understands the ideational system on which a society is based.

SYMBOLISM

While Durkheim was avowedly atheist, some of the most influential anthropologists of the later twentieth century, including Evans-Pritchard, were or became practising Roman Catholics. This is true of Mary Douglas (1921–2007) and Victor Turner (1920–83), both of whom were particularly interested in the symbolic aspects of religion. They were influenced not only by Durkheim and Evans-Pritchard, but more particularly by Durkheim's gifted pupils Marcel Mauss (1872–1950) and Henri Hubert (1864–1925), who wrote on ceremonial exchange, sacrifice, and magic.

> *Man is an animal suspended in webs of significance he himself has spun. I take culture to be those webs.*
>
> Clifford Geertz, *The Interpretation of Cultures: Selected Essays* (New York, 1973)

In her influential collection of essays *Purity and Danger* (1966), Douglas looked at the ways in which the human body is used as a symbol system in which meanings are encoded. The body is seen as a microcosm of the powers and dangers attributed to society at large. Thus, a group that is concerned to maintain its social boundaries, such as members of the Brahman caste in India, pays great attention to notions of purity and pollution as they affect the individual body. In examining purity rules, Douglas was primarily concerned with systems of classification. In her study of the Hebrew purity rules in the book of Leviticus, for example, Douglas argued that dietary proscriptions were not the result of medical or hygiene concerns, but followed the logic of a system of classification that divided animals into clean and unclean species according to whether they conformed to certain rules – such as being cloven-hoofed and chewing cud – or were anomalous, and therefore unclean and prohibited. Like Robertson Smith, Douglas observed that rituals can retain their form over many generations, notwithstanding changes in their interpretation, and that meaning is preserved in the form itself, as well as in explanations for a particular ritual action.

In the work of Mary Douglas we see a fruitful combination of the sociological and symbolist tradition of the Durkheimians and the structuralism of Claude Lévi-Strauss (1908–2009). Lévi-Strauss carried out some fieldwork in the Amazonian region of Brazil, but it is as a theoretician that he has been most influential, looking not at the meaning or semantics of social structure, but at its syntax or formal aspects. In his four-volume study of mythology (1970–81), he sought to demonstrate the universality of certain cultural themes, often expressed as binary oppositions, such as the transformation of food from raw to cooked, or the opposition between culture and nature. The structuralism of Lévi-Strauss both looks back to Russian formalism and the linguistics of the Swiss Ferdinand de Saussure (1857–1913), and forwards to more recent psychoanalytic studies of religion, both of which see themselves as belonging more to a scientific than to a humanist tradition.

RITUAL AND SYMBOL

On the symbolist and interpretive side, Victor Turner (1920–83) produced a series of sensitive, detailed studies of ritual and symbols, focusing on the processual nature of ritual and its theatrical, dramatic aspects, based on extensive fieldwork among the Ndembu of Zambia carried out in the 1950s. Clifford Geertz (1926–2006) was equally concerned with meaning and interpretation, and following a German-American tradition he looked more at culture than at social structure. Geertz saw religion as essentially that which gives meaning to human society, and religious symbols as codifying an ethos or world view. Their power lies in their ability both to reflect and to shape society.

Recently, important changes have stemmed from postmodernism and postcolonial thinking, globalization and multiculturalism. Anthropologists now often incorporate a critique of their own position and interests into their studies, and are no longer preoccupied exclusively with 'exotic' small-scale societies; for instance, there is a lot of research into global Pentecostalism and its local forms. The impact of new forms of media in the religious sphere has also become a significant area of study.

FIONA BOWIE

MYTHS AND SYMBOLS

One dimension of religions which has received particular attention by scholars has been that of myths and symbols. If we had just heard a moving piece of music, we would find it strange if someone asked us whether the music were true or false. Music, we might reply, is neither true nor false; to ask such a question is inappropriate. Most people know that music can, as it were, speak to them, even though no words are used.

As with music so with people. The question of what someone 'means' to you cannot fully be answered by saying that he is your husband or she is your wife, because there are always unspoken levels of intuition, feeling, and emotion built into relationships. The question of 'meaning' must always be seen to concern these dimensions, as well as the more obviously factual ones.

Myths

Myths take many forms, depending on the culture in which they are found. But their function is always that of pinpointing vital issues and values in the life of the society concerned. They often dramatize those profound issues of life and death, of how humanity came into being, and of what life means, of how we should conduct ourselves as a citizen or spouse, as a creature of God or as a farmer, and so on.

Myths are not scientific or sociological theories about these issues; they are the outcome of the way a nation or group has pondered the great questions. Their function is not merely to provide a theory of life that can be taken or left at will; they serve to compel a response from humanity. We might speak of myths as bridges between the intellect and emotion, between the mind and heart – and in this, myths are like music. They express an idea and trigger our response to it.

Sometimes myths form an extensive series, interlinking with each other and encompassing many aspects of life, as has been shown for the Dogon people of the River Niger in West Africa. On the other hand, they may serve merely as partial accounts of problems, such as the hatred between people and snakes, or the reason for the particular shape of a mountain.

One problem in our understanding of myths lies in the fact that the so-called Western religions – Judaism, Christianity, and Islam – are strongly concerned with history. They have founders, and see their history as God's own doing. This strong emphasis upon actual events differs from the Eastern approaches to religion, which emphasize the consciousness of the individual. Believing in the cyclical nature of time, Hinduism and Buddhism possess a different approach to history, and hence also to science.

In the West, the search for facts in science is like the search for facts in history, but both these endeavours differ from the search for religious experience in the present. In the West, history and science have come to function as a framework within which religious experiences are found and interpreted, one consequence of which is that myths are often no longer appreciated for their power to evoke human responses to religious ideas.

The eminent historian of religion Mircea Eliade (1907–86) sought to restore this missing sense of the sacred by helping people to understand the true nature of myths. The secularized Westerner has lost the sense of the sacred, and is trying to compensate, as Eliade saw it, by means of science fiction, supernatural literature, and films. One may, of course, keep a firm sense of history and science without seeking to destroy the mythical appreciation of ideas and beliefs.

Symbols

Religious symbols help believers to understand their faith in quite profound ways. Like myths, they serve to unite the intellect and the emotions. Symbols also integrate the social and personal dimensions of religion, enabling individuals to share certain commonly held beliefs expressed by symbols, while also giving freedom to read private meaning into them.

We live the whole of our life in a world of symbols. The daily smiles and grimaces, handshakes and greetings, as well as the more readily acknowledged status symbols of large cars or houses – all these communicate messages about ourselves to others.

To clarify the meaning of symbols, it will help if we distinguish between the terms 'symbol' and 'sign'. There is a certain arbitrariness about signs, so that the word 'table', which signifies an object of furniture with a flat top supported on legs, could be swapped for another sound without any difficulty. Thus the Germans call it *tisch* and the Welsh *bwrdd*.

A symbol, by contrast, is more intimately involved in that to which it refers. It participates in what it symbolizes, and cannot easily be swapped for another symbol. Nor can it be explained in words and still carry the same power. For example, a kiss is a symbol of affection and love; it not only signifies these feelings in some abstract way; it actually demonstrates them. In this sense a symbol can be a thought in action.

Religious symbols share these general characteristics, but are often even more intensely powerful, because they enshrine and express the highest values and relationships of life. The cross of Christ, the sacred books of Muslims and Sikhs, the sacred cow of Hindus, or the silent, seated Buddha – all these command the allegiance of millions of religious men and women. If such symbols are attacked or desecrated, an intense reaction is felt by the faithful, which shows us how deeply symbols are embedded in the emotional life of believers.

The power of symbols lies in this ability to unite fellow-believers into a community. It provides a focal point of faith and action, while also making possible a degree of personal understanding which those outside may not share.

In many societies the shared aspect of symbols is important as a unifying principle of life. Blood, for example, may be symbolic of life, strength, parenthood, or of the family and kinship group itself. In Christianity it expresses life poured out in death, the self-sacrificial love of Christ who died for human sin. It may even be true that the colour red can so easily serve as a symbol of

The cross is the central symbol of Christianity.

danger because of its deeper biological association with life and death.

Symbols serve as triggers of commitment in religions. They enshrine the teachings and express them in a tangible way. So the sacraments of baptism and the Lord's Supper in Christianity bring the believer into a practical relationship with otherwise abstract ideas, such as repentance and forgiveness. People can hardly live without symbols because they always need something to motivate life; it is as though abstract ideas need to be set within a symbol before individuals can be impelled to act upon them. When any attempt is made to turn symbols into bare statements of truth, this vital trigger of the emotions can easily be lost.

Douglas Davies

CHAPTER 4

The Sociology of Religion

The sociological study of religion has its roots in the seventeenth- and eighteenth-century Enlightenment, when a number of influential thinkers sought not only to question religious belief, but also to understand it as a natural phenomenon, a human product rather than the result of divine revelation or revealed truth. While contemporary sociology of religion has largely abandoned the overtly critical stance of early theoretical approaches to the truth claims of religion, the discipline retains the essential principle that an understanding of religion must acknowledge that it is, to some degree at least, socially constructed, and that social processes are fundamentally involved in the emergence, development, and dissemination of religious beliefs and practices.

METHODOLOGICAL AGNOSTICISM

While some sociologists consider that some religious beliefs are false, and that recognition of this is crucial to a sociological understanding of them, the dominant position in the sociology of religion today is that of 'methodological agnosticism'. This method states that it is neither possible, nor necessary, to decide whether beliefs are true or false in order to study them sociologically. Theology and philosophy of religion, not sociology, discuss questions of religious truth. The conditions which promote the acceptance or rejection of religious beliefs and practices, which govern their dissemination and the impact they have on behaviour and on society, can all be investigated without prior determination of their truth or falsity.

ROOTS IN INDIVIDUAL NEEDS

Theoretical approaches in the sociology of religion can usefully – if a little crudely – be divided into those which perceive the roots of religion to lie in individual needs and propensities, and those which perceive its roots to lie in social processes and to stem from the characteristics of society and social groups. The former may be further divided into those which emphasize cognitive processes – intellectualism – and those which emphasize various feelings and emotions – emotionalism.

In the nineteenth century, intellectualist theorists such as Auguste Comte (1798–1857), Edward Burnett Tylor (1832–1917), James G. Frazer (1854–1941), and Herbert Spencer (1820–1903) analyzed religious belief as essentially a pre-scientific attempt to understand the world and human experience, which would increasingly be supplanted by sound scientific knowledge. The future would thus be entirely secular, with no place for religion.

Emotionalist theorists, such as Robert Ranulph Marett (1866–1943), Bronislaw Malinowski (1884–1942), and Sigmund Freud (1856–1939), saw religions as stemming from human emotions such as fear, uncertainty, ambivalence, and awe. They were not attempts to explain and understand, but to cope with intense emotional experience.

ROOTS IN SOCIAL PROCESSES

The most influential sociological approaches that consider the roots of religion lie in society and social processes, not in the individual, are those of Karl Marx (1818–83) and Émile Durkheim (1858–1917).

For Marx, religion was both a form of ideology supported by ruling classes in order to control the masses, and at the same time an expression of protest against such oppression – 'the sigh of the oppressed creature'. As a protest, however, it changed nothing, promoting only resignation, and promising resolution of problems in the afterlife. Religion is 'the opium of the people', in the sense that it dulls the pain of the oppressed and thereby stops them from revolting. Hence, the oppressed turn to religion to help them get through life; the ruling classes promote it to keep them in check. It will simply disappear when the social conditions that cause it are removed.

> Religion is the sigh of the oppressed creature and the opium of the people.
>
> Karl Marx, *A Contribution to the Critique of Hegel's Philosophy of Right* (Deutsch-Französische Jahrbücher, 1844).

Durkheim saw religion as an essential, integrating social force, which fulfilled basic functions in society. It was the expression of human subordination, not to a ruling class, as Marx had argued, but rather to the requirements of society itself, and to social pressures which overrule individual preferences. In his famous work *The Elementary Forms of the Religious Life* (1912), Durkheim argued that 'Religion is society worshipping itself.' God may not exist, but society does; rather than God exerting pressure on the individual to conform, society itself exerts the pressure. Individuals, who do not understand the nature of society and social groups, use the language of religion to explain the social forces they experience. Although people misinterpret social forces as religious forces, what they experience is real. Moreover, for Durkheim, religion fulfils a positive role, in that it binds society together as a moral community.

MAX WEBER AND MEANING THEORY

Later theoretical approaches in the sociology of religion have all drawn extensively on this earlier work, attempting to synthesize its insights into more nuanced approaches, in which the various strands of intellectual, emotional, and social factors are woven together. A notable example is the work of Max Weber (1864–1920), probably the most significant contributor to the sociology of religion to this day. His work included one of the best-known treatises in the sub-discipline, *The Protestant Ethic and the Spirit of Capitalism* (1904–05), and three major studies of world religions.

Weber's approach to religion was the forerunner of what has become known as 'meaning theory', which emphasizes the way in which religion gives meaning to human life and society, in the face of apparently arbitrary suffering and injustice. Religion offers explanation and justification of good and of bad fortune, by locating them within a broader picture of a reality which may go beyond the world of immediate everyday perception, thereby helping to make sense of what always threatens to appear senseless. So those who suffer undeservedly in this life may have offended in a previous one; or they will receive their just deserts in the next life, or in heaven. Those who prosper through wickedness will ultimately be judged and duly punished.

RATIONAL CHOICE THEORY

The most recent, general theoretical approach in the sociology of religion, which synthesizes many previous insights, is that of 'rational choice theory'. Drawing upon economic theory, this treats religions as rival products offered in a market by religious organizations – which are compared to commercial firms – and leaders, to consumers, who choose by assessing which best meets their needs, which is most reliable, and so on. This approach promises to provide many insights. However, it has been subjected to trenchant criticism by those who question whether religion can be treated as something chosen in the way that products such as cars or soap-powders are chosen, rather than something into which people are socialized, and which forms an important part of their identity that cannot easily be set aside or changed. Furthermore, if religious beliefs are a matter of preference and convenience, why do their followers accept the uncongenial demands and constraints they usually impose, and the threat of punishments for failure to comply?

SECULARIZATION AND NEW MOVEMENTS

The sociology of religion was for many decades regarded as an insignificant branch of sociology. This situation has changed in recent years, especially in the USA. Substantive empirical inquiry has been dominated by two areas: secularization and religious sects, cults, and movements. It had been widely assumed that religion was declining in modern industrial societies and losing its social significance – the secularization thesis. This has

been questioned and found by many — especially rational choice theorists — to be wanting. The result has been intense

Hare Krishna Festival of Chariots in Trafalgar Square, London. Hare Krishna is one of many New Religious Movements.

debate. The dominant position now, though not unchallenged, is that the secularization thesis was a myth.

Central to this debate is the claim that — while religion in its traditional forms may be declining in some modern, Western industrial societies — it is not declining in all of them, the USA being a notable exception; and that novel forms of religion are continuously emerging to meet inherent spiritual needs. Some new forms are clearly religious in character. Others, it is claimed, are quite unlike religion as commonly understood, and include alternative and complementary forms of healing, psychotherapies, techniques for the development of human potential, deep ecology, holistic spirituality, New Age, the cult of celebrity, nationalist movements, and even sport. Whether such things can be considered forms of religion depends upon how religion is defined, a matter much disputed.

A second crucial element in the secularization debate is the rise of a diversity of sects and cults – the New Religious Movements – which have proliferated since the 1960s and 1970s. For the anti-secularization – or 'sacralization' – theorists, this flourishing of novel religiosity gives the lie to the thesis; while for pro-secularization theorists, such movements fall far short of making up for the decline of mainstream churches and denominations. Whatever their significance for the secularization thesis, the New Religious Movements – and sects and cults in general – have fascinated sociologists, whose extensive studies of them form a major part of the subject.

Heavy concentration on New Religious Movements has been balanced more recently by studies of more mainstream religious churches and communities, and by studies of the religious life of ethnic minorities and immigrant communities, among whom religion is often particularly significant and an important element of identity. Added to the interest in new forms of religion and quasi-religion, such studies make the contemporary sociology of religion more diverse and varied than ever.

MALCOLM HAMILTON

CHAPTER 5

The Psychology of Religion

Three key figures dominate the psychology of religion that we have inherited from the pre-World War II period: William James, Sigmund Freud, and C. G. Jung.

WILLIAM JAMES (1842–1910)

The undoubted masterpiece of the early days of the psychology of religion is the classic *Varieties of Religious Experience*, written by William James at the end of the nineteenth century. James assembled an interesting compendium of personal reports of religious experience, and embedded them in a rich and subtle framework of analysis. He thought religious experience was essentially an individual matter, the foundation on which religious doctrine and church life were built. However, from the outset his critics argued that religious experience is in fact interpreted within the framework of inherited religious teaching and shaped by the life of the institution. James hoped to put religion on a scientific basis, through the scientific study of religious experience, although he was unable to make a really convincing case for accepting religious experience at face value. Despite these issues, even his critics have never doubted the quality of his work, which is as hotly debated now as when it was first written.

SIGMUND FREUD (1856–1939)

Another important figure in the development of the psychology of religion was Sigmund Freud, although his approach was very different from that of James. Freud built his general theories upon what patients told him during their psychoanalysis, although he reported only one case study in which religion played a central part. This was the so-called 'wolf man', in whom religion and obsessionality were intertwined, which led Freud to suggest that religion was a universal form of obsessional neurosis. In fact, Freud's psychology of religion was hardly based on data at all; it was a blend of general psychoanalytic theory and his own personal hostility to religion. He wrote several books about religion, each taking a different approach. The clearest is *The Future of an Illusion*, which claims that religion is merely 'illusion', which for him is a technical term meaning wish-fulfilment.

Freud's successors have argued that what he called illusion, including religion, is in fact much more valuable than he realized to people in helping them to adjust to life.

C. G. JUNG (1875–1961)

Freud's approach to religion was continued in modified form by Carl Gustav Jung. Whereas Freud had been a harsh critic of religion, Jung was favourably disposed to it. However, his approach to religion was so idiosyncratic that many have found him an uncomfortable friend. Jung made a distinction between the ego – the centre of conscious life – and the self – the whole personality that people can potentially become. For Jung, the self is the image of God in the psyche, and the process of 'individuation' – that is, development from ego-centred life to self-centred life – is in some ways analogous to religious salvation. Jung was evasive about the question of whether there was a god beyond the psyche, and usually said it was not a question for him as a psychologist. Jung took more interest in the significance of Christian doctrine than most psychologists and, for example, wrote long essays on the Mass and on the Trinity.

Sigmund Freud (1856–1939).

> *Religious ideas … are illusions, fulfilments of the oldest, strongest, and most urgent wishes of mankind.*
>
> Sigmund Freud, *The Future of an Illusion* (London: Hogarth, 1962).

THE PSYCHOLOGY OF RELIGION TODAY

The psychology of religion went relatively quiet around the middle of the twentieth century, but has been reviving in recent decades. It has become more explicitly scientific, and most psychological research on religion now uses quantitative methods. There are currently no big psychological theories of religion, but important insights have been obtained about various specific aspects of religion. The following examples give a flavour of current work.

- *Individual differences*. One useful distinction has been between 'intrinsic' religious people – those for whom religion is the dominant motivation in their lives – and 'extrinsic' religious people – those for whom religion meets other needs. Intrinsics and extrinsics differ from one another in many ways. For example, it has been suggested that intrinsically religious people show less social prejudice than non-religious people, whereas extrinsically religious people show more.

- *Religious development.* Children's understanding of religion follows a predictable path, moving from the concrete to the abstract. However, acquiring a better intellectual understanding of religion is not necessarily accompanied by a more spiritual experience. In fact, spiritual experience may actually decline as children grow up. There have been attempts to extend a development approach to religion into adulthood. For example, James Fowler developed a general theory of 'faith development'. Although this has identified different approaches to faith in adults, it is not clear that higher levels of faith necessarily follow the earlier ones, nor that they are superior.
- *Mental health.* Despite Freud's view that religion is a form of neurosis, scientific research has shown that there is often a positive correlation between religion and health, especially mental health. It is most likely that religion actually helps to improve people's mental health, although this is hard to prove conclusively. Religion probably helps by providing a framework of meaning and a supportive community, both of which enable people to cope better with stressful experiences.
- *Conservative and charismatic Christianity.* There has been much interest in both fundamentalism and charismatic religion. One key feature of fundamentalism is the 'black and white' mindset that maintains a sharp dichotomy between truth and falsehood, and between insiders and outsiders. The charismatic phenomenon that has attracted most research interest is speaking in tongues. It seems very unlikely that this is an actual language; it is probably more a form of ecstatic utterance. One line of research has explored the social context in which people learn to speak in tongues, and another the unusual state of consciousness in which people surrender voluntary control of their speech.

Although psychology has generally taken a detached, scientific view of religion, there are other points of contact. One is the incorporation of psychological methods into the Christian church's pastoral care, begun by Freud's Lutheran pastor friend, Oskar Pfister (1873–1956). Another is the dialogue between religious and psychological world-views, an aspect of the more general dialogue between science and religion. Some psychologists consider that humans are 'nothing but' the product of their evolution or their nervous systems, whereas religious faith emphasizes their importance in the purposes of God.

FRASER WATTS

CHAPTER 6

Theological Approaches to the Study of Religion

During the development of the study of religion as a new discipline in the twentieth century, the pioneers of the field were often at pains to stress that what they did was different from theology. As such, it might be asked whether a theological approach even belongs within the study of religion. Many scholars today, who emphasize it as a scientific or historical discipline, distance themselves from any notion that theology, in any form, has a place within the study of religion. For others, the relationship is more ambiguous, while some scholars even argue that theological approaches are essential to understanding, and so truly studying, religion.

WHAT DO WE MEAN BY 'THEOLOGY'?

It is best to start by defining what we mean by 'theology' in relation to the study of religion. We will begin with some negatives. First, it does not mean a confessional approach, where the teachings of one school, tradition, or sect within a religion are taught as the true, or correct, understanding of that religion. Second, theology does not imply that there is any need for a belief, or faith content, within the person studying in that idiom. It is not, therefore, under the classic definition of the medieval Christian Anselm of Canterbury (1033–1109), an act of 'faith seeking understanding'.

We come now to the positives. First, it is about understanding the internal terms within which a religion will seek to explain itself, its teachings, and its formulations. We must be clear here that 'theology' is used loosely, because while it makes sense as a Christian term – literally it is the study of God – and can be fairly clearly applied to other theistic traditions, it is also used elsewhere to talk about broadly philosophical traditions related to transcendence. Accordingly, people use the term 'Buddhist theology' – although others question whether this usage is appropriate, but space does not permit us to engage in such disputes here. Second, it means engaging with empathy with questions of meaning as they would make sense within the religious worldview, and so goes beyond reasoning and relates to a way of life. Here, we see clear resonances with phenomenological approaches, where we seek to understand a religion on its own terms.

Anselm of Canterbury (1033–1109).

Indeed, without a theological viewpoint, it can be argued that the study of religions fails, because on the one hand it is either simply reductionist, that is to say it explains via some chosen system why the religion exists, what it does, and what it means – as tends to be the case with some parts of the sociology or psychology of religion. Or, on the other hand, it becomes merely descriptive, telling us what rituals are performed, what the ethics are, what the teachings are, how it is lived out, and so on – a simply phenomenological approach. A theological approach looks into the religion, and seeks to understand what it means to believers within its own terms, and how that system works as a rational worldview to those within it.

INSIDER AND OUTSIDER

Two important pairs of distinctions are useful to consider how theological approaches are applied. The first, developed by the anthropologist Kenneth Pike (1912–2000), and often applied to religion, concerns what are called 'emic' and 'etic' approaches. An emic approach attempts to explain things within the cultural world of the believer. An etic approach is the way an external observer would try and make sense of the behaviours and beliefs of a society or group in some form of scientific sense. Within anthropology, these basic distinctions are seen as part of the tools of the trade. Unless she enters into the thought-world of a group, culture, and society, the anthropologist will remain forever exterior, and will not understand what things mean to those in that group. Moreover, emic understandings can help inspire etic description, and assess its appropriateness. Clearly, in the study of religion, this originally anthropological distinction suggests that an emic, or theological, approach is justified.

Our second pair of distinctions is the notion of 'Insider' and 'Outsider' perspectives. These are, respectively, concepts from somebody who is a believer (an Insider), and a non-believer, that is, the scholar (an Outsider). This differs from the emic/etic distinction, because they are always perspectives of the Outsider: the scholar. As such, an emic theological approach is different from the confessional theology of an Insider. However, this distinction is often blurred. Field anthropologists speak of spending so much time within the group or society they study that they often almost become part of that group, and part of good fieldwork is about entering the life world of those studied. This applies equally to scholars of religion, especially those engaged in fieldwork.

Another issue is that scholars may be believers within a religion, and so may inhabit both Insider and Outsider worlds. This raises many interesting questions, but here we will note simply that the notion of the detached, impartial, and objective scholar is increasingly questioned. Issues raised by critical theory have suggested that every standpoint will always have a bias, and some have argued further – notably the Hindu scholar, Gavin Flood – that a religious point of view, if openly acknowledged, can form part of the broader study of religions. Moreover, religious groups are often affected by what scholars of religion say about them. Therefore, Insider worldviews and Outsider descriptions – etic or emic – become intertwined in a dance that affects each other. As such, the question of how a theological approach fits into, or works within, religious studies is far from simple.

ALWAYS 'TAINTED'?

Scholars such as Timothy Fitzgerald, Tomoko Masuzawa, and Tala Asad have argued that the supposedly secular study of religion has always been 'tainted', because it developed in a world where Christianity dominated – often with a particular kind of liberal theology – so that no study of religion is entirely free from theology. Certainly, some foundational figures, such as Mircea Eliade, had a religious worldview, and a lot of mid-twentieth century work developing the phenomenology of religion, or comparative religion, made assumptions about a religious realm that underlay all traditions. However, it is arguable whether all scholars of religion then and since are affected in this way, while a case can be made that it was not solely Christian assumptions that affected the study of religion, but that such assumptions were shaped by the encounter with various religious traditions. As such, while we must be suspicious of some categories within the study of religion, we do not need to assume that everything has a Christian basis. Indeed, Frank Whaling argues we must also not forget that many religions have a lot to say about other religions, and this leads into theorizing on comparative religion, comparative theology, and the theology of religions within a confessional standpoint which is not entirely separate from understanding a religion and its worldview.

The relationship of the study of religions and theology varies in different countries. For instance, in Germany the two tend to be starkly polarized, with theology departments being — at least traditionally — strictly confessional, normally Roman Catholic or Protestant, and the study of religions — understood as a primarily reductionist secular discipline — is always separate from theology. In the UK, the ancient universities started to admit non-Anglican Christian denominations from the nineteenth century, and so lost their confessional stance, with seminaries for training priests becoming separate or linked institutions. For this reason, it was easier to start teaching theology from a generic standpoint, which could integrate other religions as part of the curriculum, and so there are many combined departments for theology and the study of religion. The USA tends to have a more separate system, although there are places where an active study of religion discipline exists within a theology department. Obviously, such regional differences affect the way a theological approach to the study of religion is accepted or understood.

PAUL HEDGES

CHAPTER 7

Critical Theory and Religion

Our knowledge of 'religion' is always politically shaped, and never an innocent or a neutral activity. Knowledge about religion can always be questioned, and scholars of religion are finding that 'religion', and talk about 'religion', is involved with questions of power. Critical theory questions knowledge about 'religion', and reveals the social and political nature of such ideas.

DEFINING CRITICAL THEORY

Critical theory arises from a long tradition in Western thought which has questioned the truth and certainty of knowledge. It carries forward the work of the 'three great masters of suspicion', Karl Marx (1818–83), Friedrich Nietzsche (1844–1900), and Sigmund Freud (1856–1939). Following Marx, critical theory is aware that all knowledge is linked to economic and political ideology; following Nietzsche, it understands that all knowledge is linked to the 'will to power'; and following Freud, it understands that all knowledge is linked to things outside our awareness (the unconscious). The ideas of these three great thinkers influence, and are carried forward in, the work of critical theory. All three started to question the view that knowledge was neutral and rational.

Friedrich Nietzsche (1844–1900).

There are two basic understandings of 'critical theory', a strict definition and a loose definition. The former relates to the Frankfurt School of Critical Theory, an important group of German intellectuals who tried to think about society according to the ideas of Marx and Freud.

They included Theodor Adorno (1903–69) and Max Horkheimer (1895–1973), who jointly published *Dialectic of Enlightenment*, a seminal work in which they questioned Western rational thought since the Enlightenment. What did it say about the potential of human knowledge if it could lead to the ideology of Nazi Germany and the horrors of the Holocaust? Culture was understood to be formed by propagandist manipulation.

The loose definition incorporates a wider range of critical theories, which emerged – largely in France – after the student riots of 1968 in Paris. This date is a watershed in modern Western intellectual history because it reflects, among many things, a shift in the thinking about state power and the control of ideas. It was an event that brought the questions of 'power' and 'politics' to the question of knowledge and truth.

POST-STRUCTURALISM

The critical thinking that emerged in 1968 in France is known as 'post-structuralism' because it comes after an intellectual movement known as 'structuralism'. Structuralism held that one could identify a given number of structures in myth, language, and the world. Post-structuralists argued that these structures were not 'given' in the fabric of the world, but created by different societies at different points of history and in different cultures. Michel Foucault (1926–84) examined the historical nature of ideas, showing that the ways we think about the world are related to political institutions and regimes of power. Jacques Derrida (1930–2004) showed that our ways of representing the world in texts holds hidden contradictions and tensions, because language is unstable and built upon assertions of power, not truth. The instability of language refers to the discovery that the meaning of words in a dictionary simply means other words, rather than something indisputable and fixed in the world, and that meanings are simply asserted or agreed, rather than having a strong foundation given for all time. These two prominent thinkers brought knowledge under question, and enabled scholars of religion to uncover how what is and what is not classified as 'religion' can benefit certain groups of people within society. Critical theory is thus not an abstract and disengaged way of thinking, but an active ethical responsibility for the world and the way we think about the world. It shows the link between ideas and political practices.

> *Religion is a political force.*
>
> Michel Foucault

THE END OF PHENOMENOLOGY

Before critical theory, the study of religion often consisted of representing different religious traditions, and understanding them according to their rituals, beliefs, and practices. This is known as 'the phenomenology of religion', and is arguably still dominant in school and university programmes of study. Such an approach assumed that knowledge is neutral, and that different issues can be presented without too much difficulty. It was also assumed by many scholars that one does not need a 'theory' or 'theoretical position' –

a way of understanding knowledge and the world – to represent a religious tradition or a set of ideas. There was an assumption that language neutrally represented the external world according to a direct correspondence between the subject in representation (words) and the object in the external world (things) – in this case 'religious' things. However, knowledge and the categories used to represent the world and religion are now seen to be carrying hidden assumptions, with implications for gender, society, politics, colonial history, race, and ethnicity. All knowledge is now seen as reflecting a particular viewpoint or bias about the world; the production and acquisition of knowledge is never neutral. Hence, after critical theory, there is no neutral presentation of ideas about religion.

Critical theory is a way of thinking about how our dominant conceptions of religion come to be dominant or hegemonic. It seeks to identify the hidden positions within our knowledge, and to recognize that all ideas about religion hold a theoretical position about knowledge, even if that position is denied or not apparent. Critical theory offers a way of exploring 'religion' through a set of critical questions about the world and the ideas under discussion. It is not limited to the study of religion, but applies to all ways of thinking about the world, and even questions the boundary between different disciplines of knowledge. Critical theory is not a sub-discipline of religious studies – like the sociology, anthropology, or psychology of religion – but cuts across all these areas and questions all types of knowledge.

Critical theory questions the very idea of 'religion' as a Western – even Christian – category that assumes that belief is more important than how people live, which in turn is used to make assumptions about what people outside Christianity believe. This is seen as a distortion of other cultures. To correct such a view, critical theory considers traditions and cultures outside the bias of such an idea, which assumes there is something special and distinctive we can call 'religion' or 'religious'. For example, scholars question the Christian missionary interpretation of other cultures, and ask whether Hinduism is a 'religion' or the culture of South Asia. In turn, we may question whether Western capitalism is a culture or a religion. Critical theory draws attention to how knowledge is related to political ideas, and questions the domination of Western ideas (particularly European-American ideas) over other ways of seeing the world in different cultures and periods of history. It explores the way ideas powerfully rule the world and the 'truth' people have about the world.

RELIGION, POWER, AND CULTURE

Critical theory shows that the ways we think about religion are bound up in questions of power. Religious studies is now involved in exploring how the history and abuses of colonialism influenced the emergence of religion as an idea; how state power, political regimes, and the globalized world of capitalism affect this process; and how the mass media alter what we mean by religion, and uncover those activities and groups within society not recognized as religious. Critical theory exposes the abuses of power in history, and examines who benefits from thinking about the world in certain ways. It identifies those who are marginalized and unable to speak for themselves.

By examining race, gender, sexuality, and economic wealth one can see how ideas about religion often support those in power, usually the ruling educated elite of white, Western men. Thinking and writing about ideas from the position of the exploited radically changes the subject and the writing of history. Such a process questions, for example, the narrative of Christian history from its Roman-European bias, and examines Christianity through its African — particularly Ethiopian — traditions, highlighting the importance of Augustine as an African. It explores the involvement of Buddhist monks in political activism, and uncovers how the Western media distort the understanding of Islam. Critical theory also identifies ways of life outside the mainstream traditions, and explores the indigenous or local traditions around the world, which are suppressed by multinational business interests for land and oil.

Critical theory questions the boundary between religion and culture, and argues that what people do — rather than what they believe — is more important in understanding. The distinction between

Orthodox priests at a Christian festival at Timket, Ethiopia.

the religious and the secular is seen as an ideological or political tool. According to this view, the category of 'religion' can be applied to all cultural activities, such as football, shopping, fashion, club-culture, and film. The historical roots of social institutions — such as government, schools, hospitals, and law — are shown to carry ideas that can be classified as religious, even if they are not transparent. Critical theory radically alters the understanding of religion and shows the importance of the idea to world history. After critical theory, the study of religion becomes a political activity, an account of how powerful organizations in different parts of the world shape the way we understand and classify the world.

JEREMY CARRETTE

CHAPTER 8

Ritual and Performance

Like myths and symbols, ritual and performance is an area that has particularly interested religious studies scholars. Ritual is patterned, formal, symbolic action. Religious ritual is usually seen as having reference to divine or transcendent beings, or perhaps ancestors, whom the participants invoke, propitiate, feed — through offering or sacrifice — worship, or otherwise communicate with. Rituals attempt to enact and deal with the central dilemmas of human existence: continuity and stability, growth and fertility, morality and immortality or transcendence. They have the potential to transform people and situations, creating a fierce warrior or docile wife, a loving servant or imperious tyrant. The ambiguity of ritual symbols, and the invocation of supernatural power, magnifies and disguises human needs and emotions. Because rituals are sometimes performed in terrifying circumstances — as in certain initiation rituals — the messages they carry act at a psycho-biological level that includes, but also exceeds, the rational mind. Symbols and sacred objects are manipulated within ritual to enhance performance and communicate ideological messages concerning the nature of the individual, society, and cosmos. Rituals are fundamental to human culture, and can be used to control, subvert, stabilize, enhance, or terrorize individuals and groups. Studying them gives us a key to an understanding and interpretation of culture.

Anthropologists and religious studies scholars sometimes look at rituals in terms of what they do. For instance, Catherine Bell (b. 1953) distinguishes between:
- rites of passage or 'life crisis' rituals
- calendrical rituals and commemorative rites
- rites of exchange or communication
- rites of affliction
- rites of feasting, fasting, festivals
- political rituals

Another approach is to focus on their explanatory value. Mircea Eliade (1907–86) was interested in ritual as a re-enactment of a primal, cosmogonic myth, bringing the past continually into the present. Robin Horton emphasizes the reality of the religious beliefs behind ritual actions. Using the Kalabari of Nigeria as an example, he insists that religious rituals have the power to move and transform participants because they express beliefs that have meaning and coherence for their adherents. Taking a lead from Durkheim (1858–1917), other scholars claim that rituals are effective because they make statements about social phenomena. Maurice Bloch, writing about circumcision rituals in Madagascar, makes the interesting observation that because a ritual is not fully a statement and not fully an action it allows its message to be simultaneously communicated and disguised. In some cases ritual symbols may be full of resonance, as Victor Turner demonstrated for Ndembu heali ng, chiefly installation, and initiation rituals in Central Africa. In other cases the performance of the ritual itself may be what matters, the content or symbolism having become redundant or forgotten over time, as Fritz Staal has argued for Vedic rituals in India.

> *No experience is too lowly to be taken up in ritual and given a lofty meaning.*
>
> Mary Douglas

PATTERNS IN RITUAL

A key figure in the study of ritual is Arnold van Gennep (1873–1957), who discerned an underlying patterning beneath a wide range of rituals. Whether we look at seasonal festivals such as Christmas, midsummer, or harvest, or 'life crisis' rituals that mark a change in status from one stage of life to another, such as birth, puberty, marriage, or mortuary rituals, we see beneath them all the threefold pattern of separation, transition, and reintegration. Van Gennep also noted that there is generally a physical passage in ritual as well as a social movement, and that the first time a ritual is celebrated it is usually more elaborate than on subsequent occasions, as it bears the weight of change of status.

Victor Turner took up van Gennep's schema, emphasizing the movement from social structure to an anti-structural position in the middle, liminal, stage of a rite of passage. In the middle stage, initiands often share certain characteristics. There is a levelling process – they may be stripped, or dressed in such a way as to erase individuality, hair may be shaved or allowed to grow long. Neophytes are often isolated from the everyday world, and may undergo certain ordeals that bind them to one another and to those initiating them. Turner coined the term 'communitas' to describe a spontaneous, immediate, and concrete relatedness that is typical of people in the liminal stage of a rite of passage. Liminality can also be institutionalized and extended almost indefinitely, as for instance in the military, monastic communities, hospitals, or asylums.

MALE AND FEMALE INITIATION

Bruce Lincoln has criticized both van Gennep and Turner's models as more relevant to male than female initiations, pointing out that women have little status in the social hierarchy, and therefore the middle stage of a woman's initiation is less likely to stress anti-structural elements. Rather than being brought low as a prelude to being elevated, her lowlier place within society is reinforced. A woman is more likely than her male counterparts to be initiated singly, and to be enclosed within a domestic space. Women are generally adorned rather than stripped, and the nature of the knowledge

passed on during initiation is likely to be mundane rather than esoteric. Rather than separation, liminality, and reintegration, Lincoln proposes that for women initiation is more likely to involve enclosure, metamorphosis or magnification, and emergence.

Malagasy children, Madagascar.

A ritual is a type of performance, but not all performances are rituals. Richard Schechner (b. 1934) has pointed out that whether a performance is to be classified as ritual or theatre depends on the context. If the purpose of a performance is to be efficacious, it is a ritual. If its purpose is to entertain, it is theatre. These are not absolute distinctions, and most performances contain elements of both efficacious intention and entertainment. At the ritual end of the continuum we are likely to have an active 'audience', who share the aims and intentions of the main actors. Time and space are sacred, and symbolically marked, and it is the end result of the action that matters — to heal, initiate, aid the deceased, or whatever it may be. In a theatrical performance, the audience is more likely to observe than participate, and the event is an end in itself. It is performed for those watching, and not for, or in the presence of, a higher power or absent other.

FIONA BOWIE

QUESTIONS

1. What is a religion, and why can the term be problematic?

2. Why did many phenomenologists reject theological approaches to religion?

3. An atheist will always be a more objective student of religion than a believer. How far do you agree or disagree with this statement?

4. What problems might you encounter in studying a religion as an outsider?

5. What did Marx mean when he referred to religion as 'the sigh of the oppressed creature'?

6. How do Marx and Weber differ in their perceptions of religion?

7. Explain Durkheim's view of the role of religion in society.

8. Why has there been renewed interest in the sociology of religion in recent years?

9. What can psychology tell us about why people may hold religious beliefs?

10. How has Critical Theory influenced our understanding of religion since the 1960s?

FURTHER READING

Connolly, Peter (ed.), *Approaches to the Study of Religion*. London: Continuum, 2001.

Eliade, Mircea, *The Sacred and the Profane: The Nature of Religion*. New York: Harcourt, Brace, 1959.

Fitzgerald, Timothy, *The Ideology of Religious Studies*. Oxford: Oxford University Press, 2000.

Flood, Gavin, *Beyond Phenomenology: Rethinking the Study of Religion*. London: Cassell, 1999.

Geertz, Clifford, 'Religion as a Cultural System', in Michael Banton, ed., *Anthropological Approaches to the Study of Religion*, pp. 1–46. London: Tavistock, 1966.

Kunin, Seth D., *Religion: The Modern Theories*. Baltimore: Johns Hopkins University Press, 2003.

Levi-Strauss, Claude, *Myth and Meaning*. Toronto: University of Toronto Press, 1978.

McCutcheon, Russell T. ed., *The Insider/Outsider Problem in the Study of Religion*. London: Cassell, 1999.

Otto, Rudolf, *The Idea of the Holy*. London: Oxford University Press, 1923.

Pals, Daniel L., *Eight Theories of Religion*. New York: Oxford University Press, 2006.

Van der Leeuw, Gerardus, *Religion in Essence and Manifestation*. London: Allen & Unwin, 1938.

TIMELINE OF WORLD RELIGIONS

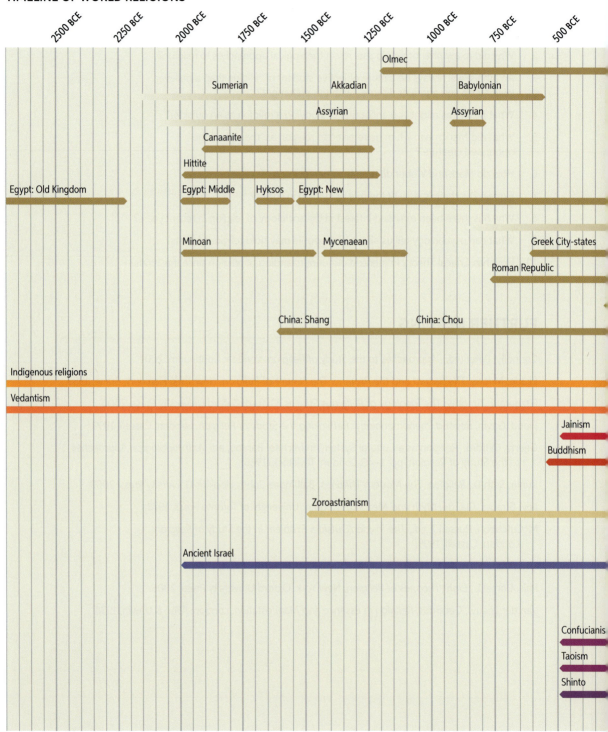

2500 BCE 2250 BCE 2000 BCE 1750 BCE 1500 BCE 1250 BCE 1000 BCE 750 BCE 500 BCE

Olmec

Sumerian　　Akkadian　　Babylonian

Assyrian　　Assyrian

Canaanite

Hittite

Egypt: Old Kingdom　Egypt: Middle　Hyksos　Egypt: New

Minoan　　Mycenaean　　Greek City-states

Roman Republic

China: Shang　　China: Chou

Indigenous religions

Vedantism

Jainism

Buddhism

Zoroastrianism

Ancient Israel

Confucianis

Taoism

Shinto

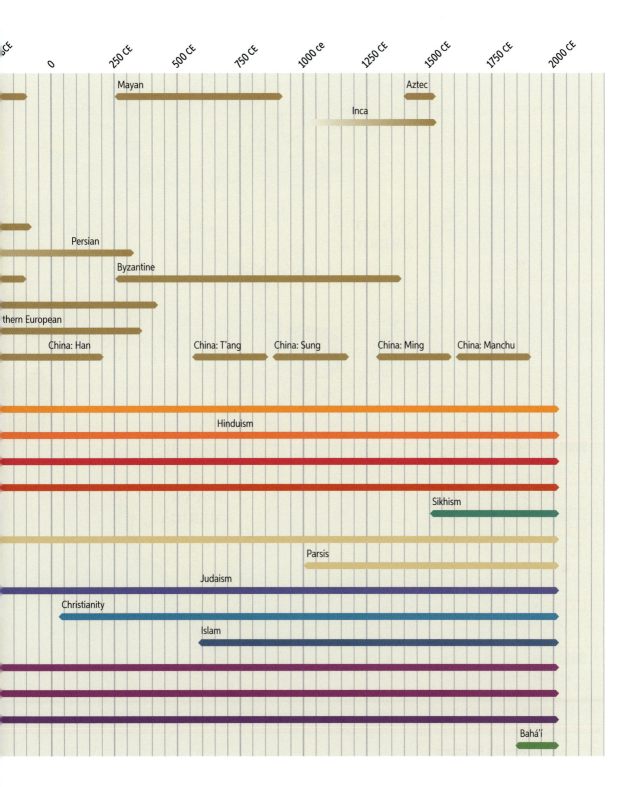

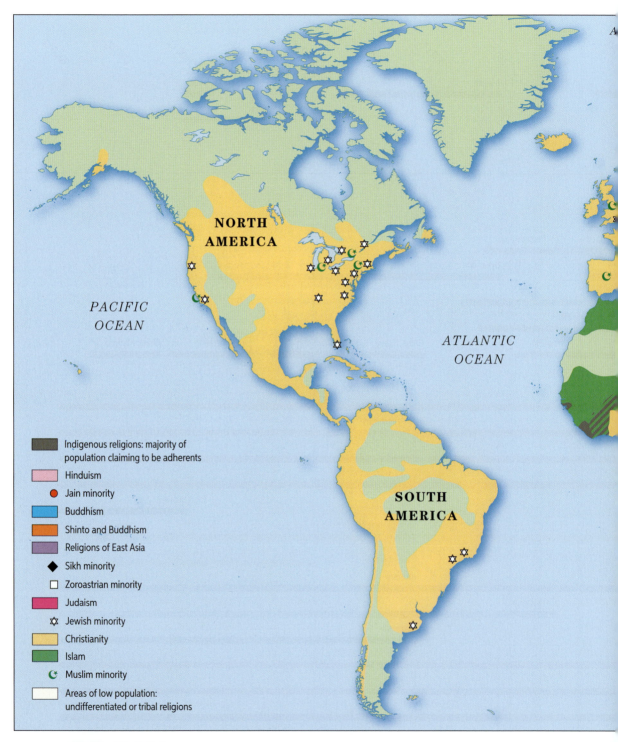

The World's Religions

A BRIEF INTRODUCTION TO JAINISM AND SIKHISM

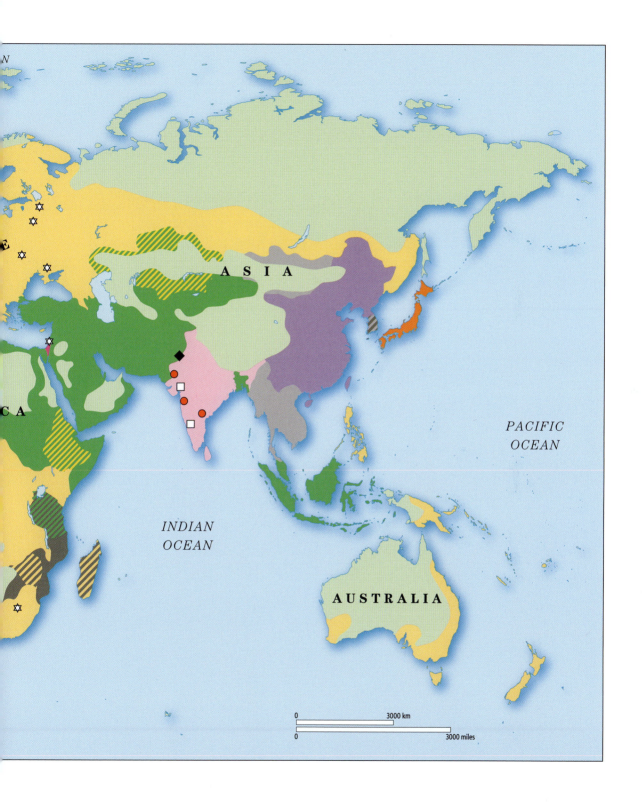

PART 2
JAINISM

SUMMARY

Jainism, like Hinduism and Buddhism, emerged from the Vedic culture of northern India, about the fifth century BCE, and is based around the teachings of Mahavira, whom Jains venerate as the twenty-fourth *jina* ('conquerer') of the last cosmic cycle. Jains hold that all living beings have a soul, and that these souls, undergoing a continuous cycle of death and rebirth, can only be liberated if the individual adopts the lifestyle of an extreme ascetic, in order to become omniscient, following the example of Mahavira himself. In the years after Mahavira's death, Jains broke into two main sects, Digambara and Shvetambara, which are divided by their views on scripture – Shvetambara Jains believe their canon descends directly from *The Twelve-limbed Basket*, the collection of Mahavira's teachings, while Digambara Jains believe this has been lost – and by the question whether there have been female *jinas*. Monasticism has an important role in Jainism, because of the value placed on asceticism, and the co-dependence of ascetics and the laity is central to the structure of traditional Jain society. Because of their belief that all living beings have souls, Jains are bound by a strict code of ethics, centred on the principle of non-violence, which forbids causing harm to any creature.

In the centuries after Mahavira's death, Jainism spread out through India, which remains its primary home to this day. Diaspora communities do exist, though these are small, and somewhat restricted by the absence of ascetics, who may travel only on foot. Alongside this, Jains – whether living in India or elsewhere – often have to compromise on some of the stricter ethical rules in order to live everyday lives in the modern world.

CHAPTER 9

A Historical Overview

Jainism originated in India, its name deriving from the term *jina* (conqueror). *Jinas* are also called *tirthankaras* – the terms are synonymous – meaning 'ford-makers'. The *jinas*, or *tirthankaras*, are religious teachers who, Jains believe, have attained enlightenment and omniscience by conquering *samsara*. Their state of omniscience means their teachings have indisputable authority, and can provide Jains with a crossing or ford – hence 'ford-maker' – from *samsara* to liberation.

Early in its history, Jainism split into two main sects: Digambara Jainism predominates in South India, Shvetambara in North-West India. Some scholars suggest the difference in beliefs and practices emerged gradually, the sects bifurcating after the Council of Valabhi, at Saurashtra, in the fifth century CE, during which the Shvetambara canon was fixed, in the absence of any Digambara representation. Today, Jainism has many different branches, most of them associated with either Digambara or Shvetambara Jainism.

THE *JINAS*

Twenty-four *jinas* are born and preach during the third and fourth phases of each half of the cosmic cycle. Jains of the Digambara sect believe all twenty-four *jinas* of the last cosmic cycle were men; Shvetambara Jains believe the nineteenth *jina*, Mallinath, was a woman. The twenty-fourth, and most recent, *jina* was called Mahavira. Jain tradition states that, just a few years after Mahavira's death, the cosmos entered the fifth phase of its regressive half-cycle, which will last for approximately 21,000 years. The first *jina* of the next group of twenty-four will not be born until the third phase of the next progressive cycle. Historians of religion sometimes associate Jainism's point of origin with the birth of Mahavira. Jains themselves subscribe to a timeless history, in which Mahavira is one of a perpetual cycle of spiritual masters. Textual evidence verifies Mahavira as a historical figure who was contemporary with the Buddha. Evidence also supports the historicity of the twenty-third *jina*, called Parshva, who lived in Varanasi about 250 years before Mahavira.

MAHAVIRA

Jain temple on Mount Shatrunjaya, near Palitana, 'City of Temples', Gujarat, India.

Mahavira lived towards the end of the Vedic period, when religious culture centred on rituals to preserve the health and prosperity of individuals, as well as cosmic equilibrium and political stability. Rituals, which sometimes involved animal sacrifice, were commissioned by high-caste householders, but performed by members of the priestly caste (Brahmans), who monopolized religious authority and had an important status in Indian society. From about the seventh century BCE, a number of 'renouncer' traditions (*shramana*) emerged. Breaking with Vedic culture, they shifted the emphasis of their religious practice from external ritual to renunciation and asceticism. Jainism and Buddhism are two examples.

Mahavira lived and preached near Patna, in the state of Bihar, and died aged seventy-two. Historians date his death at around 425 BCE; Digambara Jains believe he died in 510 BCE, Shvetambara Jains in 527 BCE. Jains celebrate five auspicious moments in Mahavira's life: his conception, birth, renunciation, enlightenment, and final spiritual liberation (*moksha*). These five auspicious events, which occur in the lives of each of the *jinas*, are thought to authenticate the *jina's* identity as a *jina*.

Mahavira's life story and teachings are recorded in Jain scriptures. The *Kalpasutra* describes how, after Mahavira's previous incarnation as a celestial being, Indra, the king of the gods, arranged for Mahavira to be transported to his mother's womb. Shvetambara Jainism tells how Mahavira was mistakenly delivered to a Brahman woman before reaching his intended mother, Trisala, who was the wife of King Siddhartha. *Jinas* are always born into the caste of warriors and noblemen, in contrast to Vedic culture, in which holy men were always Brahmans. The impact of Mahavira's renunciation is enhanced by the luxurious lifestyle that he left. Trisala had a series of auspicious dreams during her pregnancy, which were interpreted as predictions that Mahavira would be a great political or spiritual leader.

Humans and gods rejoiced when Mahavira was born. Indra took the infant to Mount Meru, at the centre of the universe, where he was anointed and consecrated. Mahavira was originally named Vardhamana ('increasing'), because his family had prospered during his mother's pregnancy. Much later he was given the name Mahavira ('great hero') in recognition of the strict asceticism he practised as an adult. Shvetambara tradition recalls that, when Mahavira was a young man, he married Princess Yasoda, who bore him a daughter. Digambara tradition denies this: when Mahavira was thirty, the gods beseeched him to pursue his destiny as a *jina*. Heeding them, Mahavira was initiated as an ascetic, the gods officiating at the ceremony. As part of his initiation, Mahavira renounced all his possessions, and even pulled the hair from his head. Novice Jain ascetics still pull the hair from their heads during their initiation ceremonies.

For the rest of his life, Mahavira wandered homeless and without possessions. Digambara tradition states he was naked from the outset. Shvetambara tradition tells how his white robe caught on a bush, and Mahavira was too deep in contemplation to notice its disappearance. He depended on alms from villagers for sustenance, although the people he encountered often abused him. He practised non-violence, undertook extreme fasting, and meditated continually on the nature of the soul. After twelve and a half years, Mahavira attained enlightenment and omniscience.

Mahavira's enlightenment is a vital moment in Jain history, because it was from this point that his career as the twenty-fourth *jina* began. The assemblies (*samavasarana*) at which he preached are depicted frequently in Jain art. Mahavira took the central position, surrounded in concentric rings by his congregation, who consisted of gods, humans, and animals. Mahavira faced east, but so that the whole congregation could hear and see him, the gods replicated his image to face each cardinal point. According to Digambara Jainism, Mahavira's body emitted a divine sound (*divyadhvani*) during his sermons, which his disciples translated for the congregation.

During his life, Mahavira is believed to have established a Jain community of 36,000 nuns, 14,000 monks, 318,000 laywomen, and 159,000 laymen. His first disciples were three Brahman priests: Indrabhuti Gautama and his two brothers, Agnibhuti and Vayubhuti, who converted after Mahavira defeated them in debate. They were soon joined by a further eight Brahman converts, bringing the total of Mahavira's closest disciples to eleven. These eleven disciples had hundreds of disciples of their own, who also converted to Jainism. Mahavira's eleven closest disciples all attained enlightenment under his guidance.

ASCETIC AND LAY COMMUNITIES

Soon after Mahavira's death, the community of Jain ascetics began to branch into groups. Having taken a vow of non-possession, they depended for survival upon alms from a laity who shared their values of non-violence and vegetarianism, and lay communities probably developed in tandem quite early. Inscriptions describing donations by tradesmen and artisans date from the beginning of the Common Era. By the fifth century CE, alms-giving had escalated from food offerings into the construction of ascetics' dwelling-halls. By the eleventh century CE, numerous ascetic communities existed, each led by a religious teacher (*acharya*), and supported by a lay following. In Shvetambara Jainism, an *acharya's* religious authority was — and continues to be — authenticated by a lineage traced back to Mahavira's disciple, Sudharman.

> *Still in meditation, [Mahavira] attained the supreme knowledge and faith, kevala by name, unsurpassed unobstructed, unlimited, complete, and full.*
>
> *Then Sramana Bhagavan Mahavira became the venerable, victor, omniscient, all-knowing, all observing.*
>
> Kalpa Sutra verses 120 and 121.

THE SPREAD OF JAINISM IN INDIA

Jains soon began to migrate from the north-east to other regions in India, ascetics to uphold their vows as wandering mendicants, the laity to pursue mercantile opportunities. Some followed a western caravan route towards Delhi, Mathura, and finally Gujarat; others followed the southern caravan route towards Orissa, Chennai, and Mysore. Mathura was an important Jain centre for trade and culture from about 100 BCE to 100 CE, perhaps even earlier; an inscription dated 157 CE at a Jain shrine here implies the shrine was already of considerable antiquity by that date. By about the fourth century CE, pressure from the ruling Gupta Empire and international trading opportunities led some Jains to travel further west to Valabhi, which became an important centre of Shvetambara Jainism.

Jain presence in South India is confirmed from about the second century BCE by inscriptional evidence at Kalinga. Digambara Jainism continued to be a major religious and cultural influence in South India for almost a millennium. By the sixth century CE, Jains were largely divided by geography and sect: Shvetambara Jains in the west, Gujarat, Rajasthan, and Punjab; Digambara Jains in the south, Maharashtra, and Karnataka. Very few Jains remained near Mahavira's homeland in the north-east.

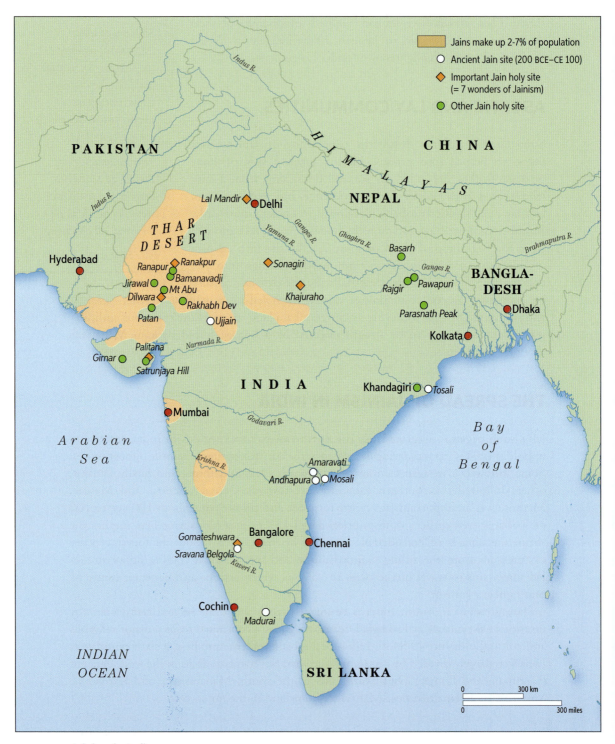

Jainism in India

ROYAL PATRONAGE

The development of Jainism benefited from periods of royal support. King Srenika, who ruled in Bihar during the period that Mahavira preached, was sympathetic to Mahavira's message. The pro-Jain Nanda dynasty, followed by the Chandragupta Maurya dynasty, ruled in Bihar until the third century BCE. In Gujarat, King Vanaraja, who had been raised by a Shvetambara ascetic, established Jainism as the state religion from 746 CE to 806. Jain ascetics sometimes forged links with royal patrons, such allegiances affording protection to Jain communities, and helping to promote Jainism. Acharya Hemachandra (1087–1172) was court scholar to Jayasimha Siddharaja, King of Gujarat (1092–1141), and to Siddharaja's heir, Kumarpala, who ruled until 1165. With Hemachandra at his side, Kumarpala employed Jain values in the running of his kingdom. He took Jain lay vows, practised vegetarianism, outlawed animal slaughter, and erected Jain temples – for example, at Taranga Hill, in Gujarat.

Digambara Jains in South India enjoyed almost seven centuries of political stability, under the rule of the Ganga dynasty in Karnataka, which came to power in 265 CE, with the assistance of a powerful ascetic called Simhanandi. Two other southern dynasties that supported Jainism were the Rashtrakutas in the Deccan, between the eighth and twelfth centuries CE, and the Hoysalas in Karnataka, between the twelfth and fourteenth centuries. During periods of royal patronage, Jainism in North and South India grew in wealth and political influence. However, by the thirteenth century, this influence began to wane, under increasing Muslim rule and the Hindu *bhakti* movement.

HERESY AND REFORM

By about the fourth century CE, the spiritual ideal of wandering Jain ascetics was jeopardized by ascetics who lived permanently in monasteries. In Shvetambara Jainism these sedentary mendicants were called *caityavasi* (temple-dwellers). Temple-dwelling ascetics questioned the religious validity of perpetual wandering, and argued that their presence preserved Jainism, by keeping Jain temples active. However, their behaviour was challenged by reformed Jains, who upheld the value of non-possession, and who regarded sedentary mendicants as lax and irreligious. In 1024 a reformed ascetic called Jinesvara Suri defeated in debate a temple-dwelling ascetic at the royal court in Patan, Gujarat. During the mid-fifteenth century, a famous layman from Gujarat called Lonka Shah established the Lonka Gaccha. These Jains sought to return to Mahavira's teachings, which, according to Lonka Shah's interpretation, meant no *caityavasi,* and no use of temples and images during worship.

During the twelfth century, an institution of clerics developed within Digambara Jainism. *Bhattarakas* ('venerable ones') underwent minimal ascetic initiation. They managed temple ritual and temple-dwelling ascetics, supervised vow-taking by the laity, maintained libraries, and oversaw lay religious education. *Bhattarakas* also acted as emissaries between Jain communities and other religious and political authorities, and, in this role, often wielded significant political influence. *Bhattarakas* are credited with negotiating political protection for Jains, and for promoting Jainism through the spread of education and publications. However, as an institution, *bhattarakas* are regarded retrospectively as an emblem of spiritual decline in Jainism, because their claim to religious authority was not verified by the moral authority of ascetic renunciation. By the early twentieth century, most of the thirty-six *bhattaraka* seats in India had become obsolete.

EMMA SALTER

LEADERS AND ENLIGHTENMENT

Indrabhuti Gautama and Sudharman were the only two of Mahavira's eleven closest disciples to survive him. Tradition tells how Indrabhuti Gautama's enlightenment was obstructed by his supreme attachment to Mahavira. He was initially distraught by Mahavira's death, but his passion ceased within a few hours, when he realized the truth of Mahavira's *moksha*, and he became enlightened too. Jains celebrate the combined events of Mahavira's *moksha* and Indrabhuti Gautama's enlightenment during a festival in November called Dipavali.

Sudharman led the ascetic community, until he too achieved enlightenment and was succeeded by his disciple Jambu, who also attained enlightenment. Early in the Common Era, Jains started to believe that, since Jambu, enlightenment was no longer possible during the current cosmic era. This protects Jainism's claim that its spiritual leaders were omniscient, because no living person's omniscience can be tested.

JAINISM TIMELINE

1000 BCE   750 BCE   500 BCE   250 BCE   0   250 CE   500 CE   750 CE   1000 CE   1250 CE   1500 CE   1750 CE   2000 CE

850–800 BCE Parshva, the legendary 23rd tirthankara

527, 510 or 425 BCE Traditional dates of death of Mahavira, 24th tirthankara

453 or 466 BCE Council at Valabhi; Shvetambara canon fixed

c 350 BCE Split begins between Shvetambara and Digambara

1089 Birth of Hemacandra, Jain philosopher and writer from Gujarat

11th–14th centuries Building of Dilwara temples on Mt Albu

17th century Beginning of Shvetambara Sthanakvasi sect

18th century Beginning of Shvetambara Terapanth sect

1970s Migration of Jains from East Africa to England

1970s Guru Chitrabhanu and Acharya Sushil Kumar go to America

CHAPTER 10

Sacred Writings

Jain sacred writings are not a tidy affair. Jainism has no single textual equivalent to, for example, the Christian Bible. Throughout Jainism's history, a variety of religious texts has become regarded as sacred: some are ancient texts, but many reflect the teachings of relatively recent saints. In Jainism, the sacredness of a text is not judged necessarily by its antiquity, but by the religious value of its content, and by its use during worship. Jains may regard as sacred writings both an ancient scripture written by an illustrious ascetic, and a nineteenth-century hymn written by a pious layman.

ANCIENT SCRIPTURES

It is not known when ancient Jain scriptures (*agamas*) were first written down. Jainism's ancient scriptural tradition began orally. Each of Mahavira's disciples is said to have compiled an oral recension of Mahavira's teachings, known collectively as the *Twelve-limbed Basket*. Early texts were written in Ardhamagadhi, a form of Prakrit, and later in Sanskrit. The current extant Jain canon was not written by a single person at a single point in history, although it is accepted by Jains as a reflection of Mahavira's teachings.

Digambara and Shvetambara Jainism do not refer to the same canon. Shvetambara Jains believe their scriptures descend directly from the *Twelve-limbed Basket*, whereas Digambara Jains believe this early literature to have been lost by the second century CE, and therefore question the authority of the Shvetambara canon. Nevertheless, some Digambara ascetics accept the authority of some Shvetambara scriptures. Possibly the migration to South India dislocated Digambara Jains from their early scriptural tradition, though some scholars suspect their rejection of Shvetambara scripture was a strategy to establish a clear division between the two sects. Evidence suggests that both scriptural traditions have the same roots.

THE DIGAMBARA CANON

The oldest text accepted by Digambara Jainism is the *Scripture of Six Parts*, which originated with the recollections of the ascetic Dharasena, who lived during the second century CE. Soon after, another ascetic, Gunabhadra, composed the *Treatise on the Passions*. These are the only two texts Digambara Jains accept as belonging to the ancient scriptural tradition; both discuss the nature of the soul and its liberation from *samsara*.

Over the centuries texts written by revered Digambara ascetics have been collated into a corpus of literature that has acquired canonical status. This is organized into four groups, known as the *Expositions*:

1. One of the most famous texts in the first group is the *Universal History*, which describes among other things the origins of Jainism and society, and the lives of Mahavira and the other *jinas*. The *Universal History* was written during the eighth century by an ascetic called Jinasena and his pupil Gunabhadra. Shvetambara Jainism has its own version of the *Universal History*.
2. The second exposition includes texts about cosmology.
3. The third exposition includes texts about codes of behaviour for ascetic and lay Jains. Some of the most important texts in this group were composed by a famous Digambara *acharya* called Kundakunda, whom some historians place in the eighth century CE, although Digambara tradition places him several centuries earlier.
4. The fourth exposition includes a broad range of metaphysical works and devotional hymns.

THE SHVETAMBARA CANON

The Shvetambara canon was formed during three councils at which senior Shvetambara ascetics — but no Digambara ascetics — recited what they could remember of the oral tradition, and their recollections were recorded and collated into textual scripture. The first council was held in Patna, 160 years after Mahavira's death; the second, 827 years after his death, was held simultaneously at Mathura, in the north, and at Valabhi, in the west. This led to some discrepancies, but Shvetambara Jains generally accepted the Mathura version as the first official canon. The third council, at which the Shvetambara canon was finally closed, was held at Valabhi, during the first half of the fifth century. The problem for scholars attempting to reconstruct the early Shvetambara canon is that no lists of the texts accepted at any of these councils remain.

The Shvetambara canon is organized into three groups:

1. The *Purva*, the tradition of lost scripture that Digambara and Shvetambara Jains accept as authoritative.
2. The *Twelve Limbs*, of which the twelfth text is lost.
3. A group divided into five categories of subsidiary texts that originate not with Mahavira's disciples, but with later ascetic teachers.

This is a broad and inclusive outline of the Shvetambara canon; not all Shvetambara Jains accept all these texts as authoritative. For example, two branches of Shvetambara Jainism, Sthanakvasi Jains and Terapanthi Jains, reject texts that advocate image worship.

Mahavira Temple, Osian, near Jodhpur, India.

TATTVARTHASUTRA

One important text accepted by both Digambara and Shvetambara Jainism is the *Tattvarthasutra*, written during the fourth or fifth century CE by the ascetic Umasvati, about whom little is known, although Digambara and Shvetambara Jains both claim he belonged to their sect. The *Tattvarthasutra* was the first significant Jain text to be written in Sanskrit, and the first to organize the main aspects of Jain doctrine into a single volume. The opening verse of the *Tattvarthasutra* identifies the essence of Jain

The enlightened world-view, enlightened knowledge, and enlightened conduct are the path to liberation.

Umasvati, *That Which Is (Tattvartha)*, trans. Nathmal Tatia (HarperCollins, 1994) verse 1.1.

doctrine as correct faith, correct knowledge, and correct conduct – a triad that became known as 'the three jewels of Jainism'.

ATTITUDES TO SCRIPTURE

Historically, only ascetics were allowed to study scripture. Laypeople were precluded, because they couldn't read the non-vernacular language of the texts, and because scriptural study without the qualification of ascetic rigour was considered dangerous. The laity encountered sacred literature at religious lectures delivered by ascetics, and through their devotional practices. Partly as a result of this, Jainism lays claim to a substantial quantity of devotional texts written by laypeople in their vernacular languages. More recently, attitudes have changed, and edited editions of some sacred Jain texts have been published, which has widened access for lay Jains and non-Jains. However, a vast corpus of sacred literature remains the exclusive domain of ascetic communities.

EMMA SALTER

CHAPTER II

Beliefs

Much of Jain doctrine is concerned with the nature of the soul, and its liberation from bondage. Every living being has a soul that is trapped in *samsara*, the continuous cycle of birth, death, and rebirth that binds a soul to its worldly existence. A soul bound in *samsara* is believed to be suffering, even if the body in which it is incarnated enjoys a happy life, because bound souls are unaware of their true nature, which is omniscience and absolute bliss. Omniscience is pure and simultaneous knowledge of all things. Once a soul becomes fully aware of its true nature, it is released from *samsara* and becomes a liberated soul — *arhat* or *kevalin* — that endures no more incarnations, and suffers no further worldly entrapment. The *jinas* were *arhats* who were distinguished by their vital roles as religious teachers.

When the physical body in which a liberated soul is incarnated dies, the liberated soul attains *moksha*, a state of absolute purity and perfection, and is called *siddha*. *Siddhas* do not have physical bodies; they reside at the topmost part of the universe, where they exist in a constant state of omniscience and bliss, and have no further dealings with mundane, worldly affairs. The soteriological goal of Jainism is to attain *moksha* and become *siddha*.

BONDAGE

Souls are trapped in *samsara* because of the effects of *karma*. In Jainism, *karma* is believed to be physical matter that permeates the entire universe, but which is so fine that it is imperceptible. Under certain conditions, *karma* 'sticks' to the soul, and obscures the soul's knowledge of its true, pure nature, as dust on a mirror prevents the mirror from giving a clear reflection. A soul generates energy by motivating the body to perform mental, verbal, or physical actions, and this energy attracts free-floating *karma* towards the soul.

Karma is unable to stick to the soul of its own accord. For this to happen, *kashaya* — which translates loosely as 'passion', and includes feelings of anger, pride, deception, and

> *The five causes of bondage are: deluded world-view, non-abstinence, laxity, passions, and the actions of the body, speech, and mind. Because of its passions, the soul attracts and assimilates the material particles of karmic bondage. The result is bondage.*
>
> *Tattvarthasutra* verses 8.1 to 8.3

greed — needs to be present. The soul produces *kashaya* in response to attachment, of which there are two types: attraction to an event or thing, and aversion to an event or thing. Eventually *karma* 'stuck' to the soul matures and produces an effect — a mental, verbal, or physical action, usually reflecting the activity by which it was attracted — before falling naturally away. This is why Jains sometimes refer to the circumstances of peoples' lives as resulting from their *karma*.

Karma sometimes produces unpleasant results, sometimes pleasing results, but — as all *karma* traps the soul in *samsara* — it is anomalous to describe any *karma* as 'good'. The action *karma* induces the soul to take generates energy that attracts more *karma* towards the soul. The soul's response of attraction, or aversion, to the action causes more *karma* to stick to the soul, and so the cycle continues. Thus, *karma* traps the soul in *samsara* because it deludes it of its own pure nature, and entangles it in a perpetual cycle of action and reaction. A soul has to be reincarnated over and over again, to expel the *karma* it has accrued, whilst at the same time continuing to accrue more *karma*. The type of *karma* accrued determines the soul's next incarnation.

LIBERATION

Jains state that the binding effect of *karma* is not the same as predestination — in which a person has no free will to affect the events of her or his life — because the soul is an intellectual force that exerts free will by the way it chooses to respond to life's events. Jains aim to control the type and quantity of *karma* attracted to their soul through their religious practices. Strategies for overcoming the mechanism of bondage therefore provide a moral framework for Jains to live by.

Jains do not depend upon an external figure of salvation, but have to take personal responsibility for their own liberation. Mahavira's teachings describe *how* Jains can cleanse their souls of *karma*, but Mahavira cannot undertake the process *for* them. The path of religious practice leading to liberation, *moksha marg*, is charted by the *gunasthanas*, fourteen stages of purity through which a soul has to pass on its way to *moksha*:

- The fourth stage is a vital turning point in a Jain's spiritual journey, because at this stage a Jain experiences *samyak darshana*, true insight. Jains interpret the experience of *samyak darshana* differently: for some, it is a deep personal commitment to their religion, for others, religious commitment coupled with a spiritual experience of communion with their soul.
- The *anuvratas* (lay vows) are taken at the fifth *gunasthana*, and the *mahavratas* (ascetic vows) at the sixth *gunasthana*. Jains believe only ascetics can attain liberation. Shvetambara Jains believe women ascetics can attain liberation, whereas Digambara Jains believe liberation can be achieved only by men.
- At the thirteenth *gunasthana*, all deluding *karma* is finally dispelled, and the soul attains omniscience.
- At the moment of death, all *karma* associated with embodiment is exhausted, and the liberated soul attains *moksha*. This is the fourteenth *gunasthana*.

Jains believe that, in this part of the universe, and during the current cosmic era, it is not possible to progress beyond the seventh *gunasthana*.

GOD AND DIVINITY

Jains do not believe in a creator-God, so Jainism is sometimes described as atheistic. This is a misrepresentation. In Jainism, liberated souls are venerated as divine being, and it is these — and most specifically the *jinas* — whom Jains worship. The hierarchy of beings worthy of veneration is expressed in the *Panch Namaskara Mantra*:

> *I bow before the* arhats
> *I bow before the* siddhas
> *I bow before* acharyas
> *I bow before ascetic teachers*
> *I bow before all ascetics*
> *This fivefold salutation*
> *Which destroys all sin*
> *Is pre-eminent as the most auspicious of all auspicious things.*

adapted from P. S. Jaini, *The Jaina Path of Purification*

The recital of this, the most popular and widely used mantra in Jainism, is incorporated into most patterns of worship, and is accepted, with small variations, by all Jain sects. The *arhats* — embodied, liberated beings — are the first to receive veneration, because they perpetuate Jain teachings. *Siddhas* have attained *moksha,* and so no longer engage in worldly affairs.

THE SOUL

Physical bodies consist of matter: they cannot act, think, or respond to the world, unless 'inhabited' by a soul, which is their sentient force. The soul is the only type of substance in the universe that has the capacity for consciousness — which is its fundamental quality. Two other qualities of the soul are energy and bliss. Only liberated souls can fully experience bliss.

Jains believe all living beings have a soul. They also believe the entire universe is permeated by infinite, minute, life monads that exist alongside more substantial life forms, such as plants, animals, humans, celestial beings, and hell beings. When a living being dies, its soul is immediately reincarnated into another body, although not necessarily of the same type. For example, a human being may not necessarily be reincarnated as another

> *Morality is perfect forgiveness, humility, straightforwardness, purity (freedom from greed), truthfulness, self-restraint, austerity, renunciation, detachment, and continence.*
>
> *Tattvarthasutra* verse 9.6

human being. Although souls are not material, they expand or shrink, to fit precisely the size and shape of their current corporeal form. Just as the light from a lamp will fill different size rooms, so a soul will fill different size bodies.

Souls are eternal, which means they can be neither created nor destroyed, and every soul is likely to have experienced every conceivable embodiment, millions of times over. Jains therefore generally adopt an attitude of respect to all living beings, in the belief that one may have been similarly incarnated in a previous life, and that most beings have the potential of becoming *siddha* in a future incarnation. Jains believe all living beings – no matter how small – have the capacity for suffering, because all living beings have a soul, and are therefore conscious. Causing harm to another soul is believed to generate an influx of *karma* to one's own soul. For this reason, Jains take great lengths to avoid harmful behaviour. Non-violence is Jainism's principal ethical value, and the emphasis Jains give to it has earned them a reputation for compassion and tolerance. Their commitment to non-violence, combined with their belief in the ubiquity of life, has resulted in many of Jainism's characteristic religious practices, such as vegetarianism. Jainism's doctrine of non-violence is said to have inspired Mahatma Gandhi in his peaceful protest for India's freedom from British rule.

COSMOLOGY

Jains believe the cosmos is uncreated and eternal. It is dualistic, consisting of consciousness, determined by the presence of souls, and that which is not conscious, which includes both matter and aspects that are neither material nor conscious, for example, space, time, motion, and non-motion.

Matter has shape, colour, taste, smell, and density. From a philosophical perspective, Jainism regards matter as both permanent and temporary. It is permanent, because the physical atoms that make up material substances are constant so can be neither created nor destroyed; at the same time it is temporary, because substances with particular qualities and modes are formed when atoms combine, but when the combined atoms dissipate, the substance they have formed is destroyed. Atoms then rejoin in different combinations, to form new substances, with different qualities and modes.

The Jain cosmos is finite in size, but vast beyond human imaginings. Its shape is sometimes described as two drums balanced on top of each other, or as a human figure, standing legs apart and hands on hips. At the base of the cosmos are seven realms of hell, inhabited by hell beings who suffer hideous tortures, as a result of the bad *karma* they have accrued during previous incarnations. Above the seven realms of hell is a middle realm, *madhya loka*, the smallest cosmic realm, and the domain of human habitation. Above *madhya loka* are seven celestial realms, inhabited by celestial beings who live in great luxury and splendour, as a result of the meritorious *karma* they have accrued during previous incarnations. At the very top of the cosmos is *siddha loka*, also known as *isatpragbhara* – 'the slightly curving place' – where liberated souls, free from *karma*, reside in a state of *moksha*.

From a soteriological perspective, *madhya loka* is the most significant cosmic realm, because it is where humans live. Liberation is only possible from a human incarnation, and then only as an ascetic. *Madhya loka* undergoes perpetual cyclical phases, like a wheel constantly rotating. There are six phases of ascent, during which *madhya loka* becomes increasingly more spiritual and human suffering decreases, followed by six phases of descent, during which spiritual purity declines and suffering increases. Twenty-four *jinas* are born and preach in *madhya loka* during the third and fourth phases of each half cycle. It is only possible to attain *moksha* during these phases, because during the other phases society is either in such a state of suffering that it cannot accept the possibility of liberation, or in such a state of contentment that it cannot accept the necessity for liberation. Jains believe our world entered the fifth phase of the descending cycle soon after Mahavira's death. Only one region in *madhya loka* – called *mahavideha*– is immune to the cycle of ascent and descent. Here a *jina* – currently Simadhar Svami – is always preaching, so *moksha* can be attained at any time. The structure and mechanism of the cosmos explains why liberation is not currently possible in our world, but encourages religious effort, by the opportunity of rebirth in *mahavideha*.

EMMA SALTER

CHAPTER 12

Family and Society

There are more than three million Jains in the world, the majority of whom live in India. Digambara Jains live predominantly in the Deccan, Delhi, East Rajasthan, and neighbouring Madhya Pradesh; Shvetambara Jains live predominantly in Mumbai, Delhi, Rajasthan, Gujarat, and Madhya Pradesh. There are also Jain communities in East Africa, Europe, and North America.

Jain religious society is organized into a fourfold structure of female ascetics, male ascetics, laywomen, and laymen, a pattern said to have been established by the first *jina*, Rishabha, also called Adinatha, and re-established by the subsequent twenty-three *jinas*. The inclusion of ascetic and lay communities in Jain religious society indicates that both communities share the same goal of spiritual liberation.

There are numerous Jain sects, most of which are associated with Digambara or Shvetambara Jainism, and have their own ascetic and lay communities. The origin of different sects often lay with reformers, who established a new ascetic lineage after a reinterpretation of doctrine or practice. For example, the seventeenth-century reformer Lavaji founded the Sthanakvasi branch of Shvetambara Jainism, when he broke from the Lonka Gaccha, because they had returned to the practice of image worship.

ASCETIC COMMUNITIES

Ascetic communities are hierarchical. The spiritual head and leader of an ascetic order is called an *acharya*. *Acharyas* and other senior ascetics may have many lay disciples, as well as their ascetic followers. Novice ascetics are at the bottom of the hierarchy. Throughout Jain history, far more women than men have taken ascetic initiation. Despite this, they are usually regarded as subordinate to their male counterparts, even if they are older, or have been an ascetic longer. Much earlier in Jain history, children sometimes took ascetic initiation. In modern times, only adults are allowed to become ascetics, and only after they have been granted permission by their next of kin.

Before initiation is permitted, a Jain layperson has to progress through eleven stages of renunciation (*pratimas*), under the supervision of an *acharya*. This includes taking five lay vows, the *anuvratas*, which are a less rigorous version of the ascetics' vows. The

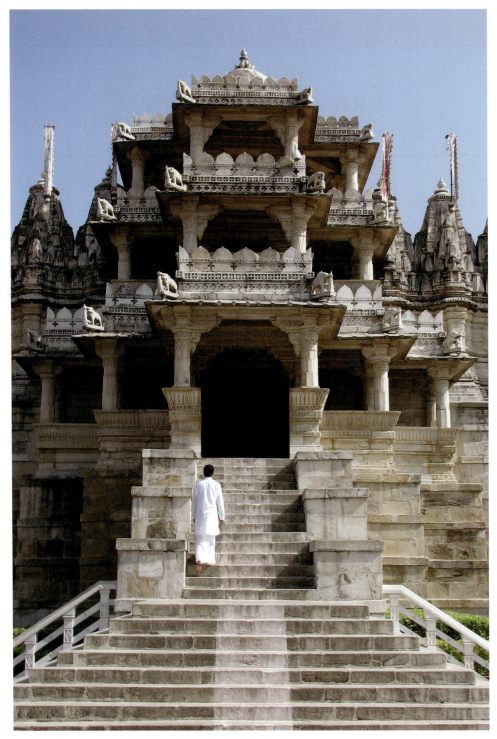

Pilgrim entering an ancient marble Jain temple, Ranakpur, Rajasthan, India.

A BRIEF INTRODUCTION TO JAINISM AND SIKHISM

ceremony at which a novice ascetic is fully initiated is called *diksha*. Lay and ascetic communities come together to celebrate and perform ascetic initiation, during which the novice wears luxurious clothes, similar to wedding finery, and is treated like royalty. This final extravagance emphasizes the material sacrifice the novice makes as she or he renounces all possessions and association with worldly life, including familial contact. The novice takes five ascetic vows (the *mahavratas*):

1. Non-violence
2. Truthfulness
3. Not taking anything that has not been given freely
4. Celibacy – fidelity for the lay Jain
5. Non-attachment to worldly possessions – restriction of wealth and possessions for the lay Jain

Finally the novice ascetic plucks the hair from her or his own head, as a symbol of commitment to the ascetic way of life. Then the new initiate undertakes a period of fasting, which is broken the first time she or he seeks alms.

To uphold their vows of renunciation, ascetics have no permanent home, and are permitted to spend only a few days in any one place. In small groups, they walk between towns and villages, where they receive donations of food from Jain laypeople. They take shelter in lodging halls (*upashraya*) built exclusively for them by the lay community. Their vow of non-violence means they are allowed to travel only on foot, because motorized transport may harm insects and other small creatures, and they cease their wanderings temporarily for the monsoon season (approximately July to October) when travelling would risk breaking their vow of non-violence, because of the proliferation of insect life. It is during this period that they have a sustained period of contact with the lay community. For this reason, many Jain festivals, in which ascetics and laypeople take part, occur during the monsoon season.

Jain ascetics renounce all worldly attachments, but do not live in solitude. Instead, ascetics are public figures, under more or less constant scrutiny by their lay followers. They have no money, and are not allowed to prepare food themselves, so they have to maintain contact with lay communities, on whom they depend for their material needs, whilst lay Jains depend on ascetics for their spiritual needs. Ascetics deliver sermons to the laity – usually from the local *upashraya* – counsel laypeople in religious matters, and administer vows of fasting and other austerities. Lay people also accrue spiritual merit by providing ascetics with food and shelter. Lay Jains regard ascetics as worthy of veneration, because they embody Jainism's doctrinal message as living paradigms of the religious ideal.

> *The universe is peopled by manifold creatures who are, in this round of rebirth, born in different families and castes, for having done various actions ... Sometimes they become nobles or outcasts and untouchables, or worms and moths, or ... ants.*
>
> Uttaradhyayana Sutra, That Which Is (Tattvartha), trans. Nathmal Tatia (London: HarperCollins, 1994).

LAY COMMUNITIES

Jain lay society is divided by sect and caste. Interaction and intermarriage between Jains of different sects is rare in India, although it is more frequent amongst diaspora communities, because of a greater need for solidarity. In India, intermarriage between Jains and Hindus of the same caste is not uncommon. The Jain marriage ceremony and funeral rites are similar to their Hindu equivalent. Jains believe religious qualities are judged by a person's conduct, not by their birth status, so caste division is restricted to a secular, societal role. However, in practice many Jain sects prohibit low-caste Jains from taking ascetic initiation. Sthanakvasi Jainism is an exception.

Commitment to non-violence means that Jains are prohibited from entering professions associated with causing harm to other living beings. For example, a Jain would never operate a slaughterhouse, or trade in leather goods. Apart from this restriction Jains enter all types of professions. In India many are traders or financiers.

In modern times, it is rare for lay Jains to take lay vows, unless they intend to initiate as mendicants in the future. Nevertheless, the practice of non-violence is a strong influence in their daily lives. Jains are vegetarian, and many also avoid eating potatoes, which they believe to contain millions of tiny life-forms, and root vegetables, because harvesting them may cause harm to earth-dwelling creatures. Jain households tie small muslin bags over their taps to filter their water, to avoid ingesting and harming water bodies. Jains living in countries where tap-water is not fit for drinking boil and re-filter their water for health purposes. Non-violence also extends to proactive endeavours, such as charitable donations.

EMMA SALTER

CHAPTER 13

Worship and Festivals

In Jainism, worship is directed towards ascetics, because their commitment to renunciation and non-violence is thought to represent the religious ideal taught by Mahavira and the other *jinas*. Lay Jains venerate ascetics, and ascetics venerate their superiors. The *Panch Namaskara Mantra*, which is recited by ascetic and lay Jains, venerates all ascetics, from the novice to the liberated soul. Ascetics are believed to have progressed further along the path of liberation — *moksha marg* — than lay Jains, and therefore to have attained a higher level of spiritual purity.

Whenever a lay Jain meets an ascetic, whether at a public sermon or private interview, she or he performs a rite of veneration, *guru-vandan*, bowing twice to the ground before the ascetic, and reciting a short prayer of veneration. Often the ascetic will then offer a blessing. Devout Jains visit ascetics' lodgings daily to perform *guru-vandan*. Theoretically, lay Jains do not personalize their veneration towards one particular ascetic, because all Jain ascetics are equal representatives of Jainism's religious ideal; in practice, they sometimes revere a particular ascetic as their special guru.

VENERATION OF THE *JINAS*

The twenty-four *jinas* were perfect, liberated ascetics, who taught the path of liberation, and attained *moksha*, and are thus the principal focus of worship. Jains worship the *jinas* during rituals called *puja*, and also express their veneration of them in a rich tradition of devotional songs.

Shvetambara Jains of the Terapanthi and Sthanakvasi sects, and Digambara Jains of the Taranapanthi sect, do not use images of the *jinas* during worship, as they do not believe the practice to have been sanctioned by the *jinas*. Ascetic and lay Jains who belong to these sects perform their worship in plain halls, usually attached to the ascetics' lodgings, venerating the *jinas* through *mantra* chanting, meditation, and scriptural study. If available, a senior ascetic teacher may provide a focal point; otherwise a scriptural text may be used as a substitute. In either case, it is the *jinas'* teachings that are the focus of veneration.

Other Shvetambara and Digambara sects use images of the *jinas* during their worship. Usually crafted in marble or metal, they depict the twenty-four *jinas* as identical to each

other; with robust male physiques, broad shoulders, and narrow waists — always meditating, either sitting or standing. A symbol carved at the base

Stone statue of an elephant outside the ancient Jain temple of Indra Sabha, carved out of solid rock, at Ellora Caves, near Auranabad, India, between the fifth and tenth century CE.

of each image identifies which *jina* it represents: for example, images of Mahavira are identified by a lion, whilst images of Parshvana — the twenty-third *jina* — have a canopy of cobra hoods. Digambara images are plain and naked, depicting the *jinas* in their ascetic role; Shvetambara images depict the *jinas* as nobility, before they became ascetics, and so are bejewelled, dressed in royal regalia, and adorned with gold or silver crowns. A Digambara or Shvetambara temple is often very ornate and beautiful, and usually dedicated to a single *jina*, an image of whom is the focal point. Large temples may also house images of other *jinas* and associated deities.

Most ritual worship in the temple is non-congregational. One simple ritual — *darshan* — involves gazing upon the image of a *jina* with a feeling of devotion and humility. Another ritual — *aarti* — is usually performed in the evening, and involves placing five small candles — representing five different types of knowledge — on a special tray. Worshippers then wave the tray in clockwise, circular motions before the image, while singing devotional hymns. Another ritual many Jains perform daily is the '*puja* of eight substances'.

As liberated beings, who have transcended worldly affairs, the *jinas* take no reciprocal role during worship. Worship does not appease them, nor do they respond to it by granting favours. Despite this, Jains feel immense love and devotion towards the *jinas*. The most important aspect of Jain worship is the devotional sentiment of the worshipper, regardless of ritual patterns, and whether or not an image is present. For this reason, Jains have to perform their own worship; no one else can do it on their behalf. Substances used during rituals are not offerings from the worshipper to the *jinas*, who have no use for them, but gestures of renunciation on the part of the worshipper. This is one reason why ascetics cannot perform temple rituals; they own nothing, and therefore have nothing to renounce.

FESTIVALS

Festivals are a time when lay Jains worship collectively, and often lay and ascetic communities come together. Most Jain festivals celebrate an aspect of the lives of the *jinas*: for example, *Mahavira Jayanti* in March/April celebrates Mahavira's birthday. Jains share some festivals with Hindus, and in mid-October celebrate *Diwali*. For Jains, however, *Diwali* signals the start of a new ritual and commercial year ,and celebrates Mahavira's transcendence to *moksha* and the enlightenment of his disciple Gautama.

PARYUSHAN

Paryushan ('abiding') is an important Shvetambara festival, closing the old year. It occurs in August/September, and lasts for eight days. Jains may attend the temple more often than usual, and some observe fasts, ending in a celebratory feast on the last

THE PUJA OF EIGHT SUBSTANCES

This ritual varies slightly between Jain communities, and is usually performed in the morning after bathing.

- Upon entering the temple, the worshipper bows before the *jina* image, while saying *nisihi* ('abandonment'), signifying that she or he has left the mundane world and entered the sanctity of the temple.
- The worshipper then circumambulates the image three times clockwise.
- Shvetambara Jains anoint the image with milk mixed with water, and, while reciting special prayers, use the third finger of their right hand to apply camphor and sandalwood paste to nine parts of the image in the following order: left and right big toes, right and left knees, right and left wrists, right and left shoulders, crown, forehead, throat, chest, and navel. Digambara Jains do not touch their *jina* images, so for this part of the ritual they sit before the image, pouring water – or a mixture of milk and water – from one vessel into another, and reciting prayers.
- Shvetambaras and Digambaras place a fresh flower by the image, and, in a circular motion, waft incense, followed by a camphor lamp.
- The worshipper then performs a joyous dance before the image, while waving a yak-tail fan.
- Next, the reflection of the *jina's* image is observed in a hand-held mirror.
- The worshipper then places a handful of dry rice on a special plate, forming it into the shape of a swastika, representing four possible incarnations: human, animal, celestial being, or hell being. Some food – usually sweets, fruit, or nuts – and sometimes a small amount of money, is placed on top of the rice swastika.
- At the end of the ritual, the worshipper says *nisihi* again, perhaps spends some time in spiritual contemplation, and usually sounds a bell upon departure.

> *The observer of vows should cultivate friendliness towards all living beings, delight in the distinction and honour of others, compassion for miserable, lowly creatures and equanimity towards the vainglorious.*
>
> Tattvarthasutra by Umasvati chapter 7 verse 6.

day of the festival. Fasting is an important and frequently performed religious practice amongst Jain laity. It is usually women who fast, men often claim to be restricted by their professional obligations. In addition to spiritual benefits, the completion of an arduous fast may improve the social prestige of the family of the person fasting. Pious lay Jains may stay at the mendicants' lodgings, having taken temporary vows of asceticism, and others make a pilgrimage to a holy site, such as Mount Shatrunjaya, in Gujarat, or Shravana Belagola, in Karnataka.

Ascetics deliver sermons daily for the first three days of *Paryushan*, and twice daily for the remaining five days. On the fourth to seventh days, this involves a public reading of the *Kalpasutra*, the Shvetambara scripture containing histories of the twenty-four *jinas*. The description of Mahavira's birth, on the second day of the reading, is accompanied by an elaborate ritual and great celebration.

On the final day, Jains perform *pratikraman*, a congregational ritual that is a communal statement of atonement and repentance for any harmful actions that may have been committed during the year. For more pious Jains, *pratikraman* is also a daily practice. At the end of *Paryushan*, many Jains send cards or emails to relatives and friends, seeking forgiveness for any wrong-doing. A devout Jain carries no grudge or quarrel over into the new year.

The equivalent Digambara festival is called *Dashalakshanaparvan* ('Festival of Ten Religious Qualities') and lasts ten days. The ten chapters of the *Tattvarthasutra* are recited publicly, with laypeople taking an active role, as there are relatively few Digambara ascetics. Towards the end of the festival, a special *puja* with flowers is performed to Ananta, the fourteenth *jina*. On the last day, rites of atonement are performed, similar to those of *Paryushan*.

ASCETIC PRACTICES

By taking ascetic initiation, a Jain dedicates her or his life to spiritual progression. The vows of renunciation ascetics take mean they no longer have a secular role in society; their worldly possessions are replaced with those things necessary for their ascetic lifestyle. For Digambara ascetics, this is a broom made from naturally shed peacock feathers and a water pot. They do not wear robes; *Digambara* literally meaning 'sky-clad', that is, naked. It is socially unacceptable for women to be 'sky-clad', which is one reason Digambaras – unlike Shvetambaras – do not accept that women can attain liberation. Shvetambara ascetics receive a set of simple white robes, a bowl for collecting alms, and a broom made from naturally shed cow-tail hair. As well as relinquishing worldly possessions, renunciation also means giving up anything that may be pleasing to the senses, such as tasty food, or comfortable living quarters.

Ceiling of the marble Jain temple at Ranakpur, Rajasthan, India, dedicated to Adinatha.

I AM A JAIN

I am a Jain nun, and have been practising Jainism for nineteen years. I joined my monastery when I was eighteen. Jain ascetic life is very simple: I have two sets of clothes; I eat pure vegetarian food in handmade wooden bowls; I have no monetary assets – no property, no bank balance; I have given up family attachments; and I am happy, having no desires for material possessions.

I did not become a nun because I was unhappy. I had incredibly happy moments with my parents, my two sisters and brother. I was born in Chennai, in southern India. My father is a physician and radiologist, my mother a housewife. We always said prayers and meditated for an hour on Sunday. The inspiration of my family, and the religious environment in which I was brought up, made a deep impression on me and developed within me. My parents are not only followers of the Jain religion, but have applied Jain principles throughout their lives. Their deep spirituality and religious commitment influenced me a lot.

Eventually I started to learn more about Jainism, by discussing and spending time with many Jain monks and nuns who visited Chennai. Their simple way of life appealed to me. After finishing my education at high school, I sought the permission of my parents to join the training institution for nuns. I had to wait a couple of years, to convince my parents of my commitment to the religious life: they needed to be sure this was what I really wanted. I wanted a life that was peaceful, purposeful, productive, and progressive. I wanted

something special, that gave me a feeling of contentment and fulfilment. Finally, I chose this path. In the Jain training centre, I read not only the holy scriptures, but also comparative studies of different religions, philosophies, and ideas. I studied for a Master's degree in comparative religion and philosophy at the Jain Vishwa Bharati Institute at Ladnun, in Rajasthan. This period of study helped me to understand my beliefs and values with more clarity.

After six years of training, my spiritual gurus, Acharya Tulsi and Acharya Mahaprajna, initiated me, at a gathering of thousands of people. It was a deeply spiritual celebration. I took vows of non-violence, truth, non-stealing, celibacy, and non-possession. It is a lifelong commitment, with self-discipline and self-control. That day I was so happy – my dream was coming true. I was at the feet of my guru, receiving blessings for this new journey of spiritual enlightenment. I was dressed in a white robe and my head was shaved. I was named 'Samani Charitra Prajna'.

Acharya Tulsi and Acharya Mahaprajna established the Saman Order in 1980. Their vision was to propagate and reinforce the message of non-violence, peace, and harmony throughout the world. In Jainism, we believe that water, air, fire, earth, and plants are living beings. Although it is not possible to be completely non-violent, we try to prevent unnecessary violence by our actions, words, and thoughts. Acharya Tulsi established a new form of monastic life. The lifestyle of a *saman* or *samni* is very similar to that of a monk or nun in other Jain monastic communities, but there are differences. For example, we use transport to educate and enhance human life and values at the global level.

As a *samni,* my lifestyle is totally different from that of a secular person. I spend four to five hours a day in meditation, prayer, chanting, and reading the holy scriptures. Twice a day, before sunrise and after sunset, I recite a special prayer known as *pratikraman,* in which I ask for forgiveness from, and give forgiveness to, all living beings; if I have committed sins, or violated any kind of vows, I repent and resolve not to repeat them. I freely admit my flaws and mistakes, and seek to improve myself.

I observe *preksha* meditation every day. A scientific technique, it is aimed at transforming my inner personality; it is known to have an impact on the endocrine system, by changing the biochemicals and balancing the hormones. It helps me a lot, enabling me to eliminate negative emotions and regenerate positive qualities, and benefits me by relaxing me and giving me peace of mind. As a *samni,* I do not eat and drink before sunrise or after sunset. This has a basis in science, as it has been shown sunlight is needed for good digestion.

Along with the daily practice of meditation and prayer, once a year I celebrate eight special days of spiritual enhancement and uplifting of my soul. This is called *paryushan* – 'being closer to your soul' – and is practised not only by monks and nuns, but by the whole Jain community. We listen to sermons, fast day and night, and practise living simply, with detachment from the material world and self-control. The last day of *paryushan* is very important, because this is the day when we recall all our past mistakes and sins, ask forgiveness from those against whom we have sinned, and give forgiveness to those who have sinned against us.

Jainism emphasizes a process of self-purification. All my efforts are focused on freeing the soul from the bondage of *karma.*

As a *samni,* ten months a year I travel extensively in India and overseas, lecturing at universities, colleges, national and international conferences, and to various associations. I have often participated in interfaith dialogues and discussions, and have conducted many camps, workshops, and seminars on stress management, anger management, the science of living, and ailments such as diabetes, high blood pressure, anxiety, obesity, allergies, and heart attacks. The rest of my time I spend in the presence of my guru, whose holy presence clarifies many doubts and queries.

I am very happy I have dedicated my whole life to a good cause, and to be following the message of non-violence, and a soul-oriented religion that emphasizes human values.

Samani Charitra Prajna

Of the five ascetic vows, the most famous is commitment to non-violence: not harming any creature – however small or seemingly insignificant – by action, speech, or thought, and not condoning such actions by others. Ascetics use their broom to sweep gently the ground before them free from insects, so they do not tread on them. During the rainy season, they do not travel, because the risk of harming creatures is too great. Terapanthi and Sthanakvasi Shvetambaras wear cloth mouthshields, to protect tiny airborne creatures from being harmed by their breath. During alms collection, donations are accepted only if they meet the ascetics' strict ethical requirements, food being inspected for insects and other impurities prior to consumption. Collecting or eating alms after dark is prohibited, because cooking-fires may lure insects to their deaths. Jain commitment to non-violence also includes honesty, respect, and compassion towards others.

Ascetic practices, which can be internal or external, are believed to 'burn off' *karma* already attached to the soul. Internal practices develop spirituality, and are met by the six obligatory actions. External practices involve enduring physical hardships. The most frequently performed is fasting, which includes total abstinence from food for a designated period, reduction – for example, eating every other day – or denial of certain types of food. The most dramatic form is *sallekhana* (elective fasting until death). The ascetic meditates throughout, to maintain a state of equanimity, which is believed to result in a meritorious rebirth. Ascetics are permitted to perform *sallekhana* only if they are already facing death by terminal illness or old age, and the process must be overseen by a senior ascetic. Few perform *sallekhana*, but those who do are highly celebrated.

EMMA SALTER

CHAPTER 14

Jainism in the Modern World

Jainism is a dynamic religion, remaining relevant in the modern world, by responding to social change, and to scientific and technological innovations. Some Jains embrace modernization, while others prefer to uphold established traditions; the different points of view have sometimes led to tension within the Jain community. The estimated 100,000 Jains living outside India face additional challenges, in that Jain ascetics play a vital role in the religious practices of Jain laypeople, yet are allowed to travel only on foot, and not permitted to travel outside India.

SOCIAL CHANGE AND MODERNIZATION

Changing social values have influenced traditional Jain practices. For example, most Jain sects no longer allow children to take ascetic initiation. Jains sometimes attempt to demonstrate the validity of Jain doctrine by reference to current social issues, such as associating vegetarianism with healthy living, or associating non-violence with cultural tolerance.

Jainism has also responded to scientific discoveries. Some Jains have suggested science proves the truth of Jain doctrine and, therefore, the authority of the *jinas*, because Jain teachings about the formation of matter from particles correspond with scientific discoveries about atoms. Where science and doctrine are not reconciled, as with the structure of the cosmos, Jains have to decide whether to accept scientific discovery and reclassify their doctrinal beliefs as mythical, or reject scientific discovery and hold fast to their doctrinal beliefs.

Technological advances have presented Jains with new ethical dilemmas. Some progressive mendicants use microphones during their sermons, to ensure the entire congregation can hear them; while other mendicants refuse to use electrical equipment, out of concern that electricity may harm tiny airborne creatures. Advances in printing, publishing and information technology have made Jain literature increasingly accessible to a broad readership that includes lay Jains and non-Jains. Some Jains hope this will further the understanding of Jainism, while others are concerned that sacred texts may be misinterpreted, or treated irreverently. Modernization also obliges Jains to rethink the motivation behind certain religious practices. For example, today most lay Jains live in houses or apartments where it is no longer appropriate to suggest eating after dark increases the risk of harming insects. If they do not eat after sunset, they have to justify this as exercising discipline and respect for tradition, rather than as an act of non-violence.

Today many Jains are well educated; religious rituals that appear to hold little meaning beyond tradition may not satisfy them. However, numerous independent educational programmes are being established in India and abroad, to teach lay Jains about Jainism, and revitalize their commitment, by explaining the doctrinal reasons for their religious practices. The first Jain university was established in 1970 at Ladnun, Rajasthan, under the direction of Acharya Tulsi (1914–97).

THE JAIN DIASPORA

Towards the end of the nineteenth century, many Indian people emigrated to East Africa, where they established homes and businesses. By 1926, a Jain temple had been built in Nairobi, Kenya, and another was constructed in Mombasa in 1963, indicating the religious community's growth. However, during the late 1960s and 1970s, Indian people were persecuted by East African political regimes, and many fled to Britain and North America, where they took up citizenship, while endeavouring to establish a communal identity.

To Jains who do not live in India, the absence of ascetics presents a difficulty, since ascetics have religious authority, and play a vital role in the religious practices of Jain laypeople, offering instruction, administering vows, performing initiation and consecration ceremonies, and giving laypeople the opportunity to gain spiritual merit through alms-giving. Some diaspora Jains travel to India, either regularly or occasionally, to be in the presence of

MODERN JAIN LEADERS

Shrimad Rajachandra (1867–1901) was a Jain layman and guru from Gujarat who taught the importance of devotion to an authoritative guru for achieving liberation. His followers turn to spiritual laypeople instead of to ascetics. As lay gurus have no travel restrictions placed upon them, the Shrimad Rajachandra movement has transferred well to diaspora communities.

Kanji Swami (1889–1980), also from Gujarat, was initiated as a Sthanakvasi ascetic in 1913. He later relinquished his ascetic status to become a Digambara layman, although he never married. Kanji Swami attracted a huge following, which is one of the most successful movements in modern Jainism. Like the Shrimad Rajachandra movement, the Kanji Swami Panth is a lay organization that places little emphasis on the role of ascetics, and therefore has an important place among diaspora Jains.

Acharya Mahaprajna (1920–2010), who succeeded Acharya Tulsi as spiritual leader of Terapanthi Jainism, instigated numerous reforms, and established a class of 'semi-ascetics': partially-initiated men and women who may travel abroad to teach and administer to lay Jains.

Chitrabhanu (b. 1922) was a Shvetambara ascetic in India who relinquished his status and settled in North America in the 1970s, establishing an extensive community of lay followers, who regard him as an authoritative guru.

It doesn't matter if you become a Jain, aspire to become a good man, a moral person.

Acharya Tulsi

ascetics, though family, work, and financial restraints make such trips difficult for many. This difficulty is compounded by ascetics being peripatetic for eight months of the year. Some modern movements have — consciously or not — addressed the problem of ascetic absence. Terapanthi Jainism, the followers of Chitrabhanu, Shrimad Rajachandra, and Kanji Swami all have different organizational structures, but each is an example of progressive and modernized Jainism.

EMMA SALTER

QUESTIONS

1.   What is the role of a *jina*?

2.   Explain the main points of disagreement between Digambara and Shvetambara Jains.

3.   Why is asceticism so important in Jainism?

4.   Explain why Jains do not believe enlightenment is possible during the current cosmic era.

5.   Why is the Digambara scriptural canon so much smaller than the Shvetamara canon?

6.   Explain the Jain conception of *karma* and its role in trapping a soul in *samsara*.

7.   Why do Digambara and Shvetambara Jains have different views about the role of women?

8.   Why do Jains have such a strong position on non-violence?

9.   What attracts Jains to an ascetic lifestyle?

10. Why does modern life pose so many problems for strict Jains?

FURTHER READING

Carrithers, Michael, and C. Humphrey, *The Assembly of Listeners: Jains in Society*. Cambridge: Cambridge University Press, 1991.

Cort, John E., *Jains in the World: Religious Values and Ideology in India*. New York: Oxford University Press, 2004.

Dundas, Paul, *The Jains*. New York: Routledge, 2002.

Jaini, Padmanabh, *The Jaina Path of Purification*, 2nd ed. Columbia, MI: South Asia Books, 2001.

Laidlaw, James, *Riches and Renunciation: Religion, Economy, and Society among the Jains*. New York: Oxford University Press, 1996.

Vallely, Anne, *Guardians of the Transcendent: An Ethnography of a Jain Ascetic Community*. Toronto: University of Toronto Press, 2002.

PART 3
SIKHISM

SUMMARY

Of the world's major religions, Sikhism is one of the youngest. Around 1500, Nanak, the religion's founder, is said to have been transformed by God while bathing, and emerged with the words 'There is no Hindu, there is no Muslim' – a simple creed which formed the basis for Sikhism. Reflecting this idea, Sikh scripture begins by emphasizing the unity of God and his creation. Accordingly, believers are encouraged to accept all religious traditions, and to treat all humanity with equal respect – radical notions in sixteenth century Punjab, riven by conflict between Hindus and Muslims, and dominated by the social restrictions of the caste system. *Karma* and the cycle of life – *chaurasi* – are important in Sikhism: in order to escape the punishment of rebirth, one must aspire to the Guru's example. This is not achieved by asceticism, however, since the Guru was a married man, who fulfilled his obligations to both family and community. After Nanak, a line of ten Gurus, who consolidated his legacy, led Sikhism. During this period, Sikhism's primary scripture, the *Adi Granth*, was compiled, from the work of the first five Gurus. In the era of the tenth – and last – Guru, the *Adi Granth* was itself instituted as a Guru, while the *Khalsa*, the community of the initiated, was founded.

Sikhism's early development was in a Muslim kingdom. In time, Sikhs would establish their own short-lived state; but during the nineteenth and twentieth centuries had to exist under British rule, and then within the largely Hindu secular Indian republic. In the late nineteenth century, the Sikh reform movement emerged, to reassert the religion's distinct identity, which many feared was being lost. The last decades of the twentieth century saw the rise of a Sikh-Punjabi nationalist movement, which inevitably resulted in significant conflict with the Indian state, most notably during the 1980s. A significant and vocal diaspora community meanwhile has grown in the West, as a result of post-war migration.

CHAPTER 15

A Historical Overview

The history of Sikhism has always been closely linked to the Punjab, the land of its origins, because of its situation in the north-west of the Indian subcontinent, always the first region of the fertile northern plains to be exposed to successive conquests by invaders crossing the great mountain boundaries through such routes as the Khyber Pass. The first such cultural inroads recorded were those of the Aryan tribes in the Vedic period, which initiated the beginnings of the Hindu tradition. The last were the invasions mounted by Muslim sultans from Afghanistan and Central Asia from early in the first millennium CE, which resulted not only in the establishment of centuries of Muslim rule over the Punjab, but also in the presence of substantial numbers of Muslims in Punjabi society, largely the product of peaceful conversion.

When Sikhism first emerged, some five hundred years ago, it appeared in a society already religiously divided. It would be quite misleading to think of Sikhism as a mechanical combination of Hindu and Muslim elements, since from its beginnings it has been self-defined as a new and independent third way. Equally, its evolution needs to be understood as a complex process of the ongoing relationship, within the Punjab and beyond, of a vigorous minority community to the two numerically larger traditions of Hinduism and Islam.

GURU NANAK

Nanak (1469–1539) is revered by all branches of the religion as the defining first Guru of the *Sikhs* (Punjabi for 'disciples'). He was by birth a Hindu of the Khatri caste — professionals with strong hereditary links to the administration — and his father was a village accountant. Nanak himself was married with a family, and had a career as an administrator working for a local Muslim nobleman. His mission began when he was around the age of thirty, with a transforming experience of the divine reality, granted to him when he entered the river to bathe. Mysteriously hidden from the view of his companions, he emerged after three days, uttering

> *Great Guru whose encounter brought the Lord to mind!*
>
> *With his teaching as their salve, these eyes survey the world.*
>
> *Attached to the other, some traders left the Lord and roamed.*
>
> *How few have realized the Guru is the boat,*
>
> *Which delivers those he favours safe across.*
>
> Adi Granth 470.

the words 'There is no Hindu, there is no Muslim,' taken as the inaugurating formula of the new religion. Nanak then embarked upon an extended series of travels, before returning later in his life to the Punjab, where he established a settled community of the first Sikhs.

Guru Nanak's teachings are embodied in his verses, hymns, and longer poetical works, which now form a substantial collection at the heart of the Sikh scriptures. In their broad thrust, these teachings are similar in content to those of other North Indian teachers of the medieval period from lower castes, such as Kabir (1440–1518) and Ravidas. They all preached that salvation was dependent upon devotion not to a divine incarnation, such as Krishna, but to the undifferentiated Formless One; and that to observe caste practices and Brahmanical authority was as futile for those who wished to be saved as obedience to the alternatives promulgated by Islam. But the subsequent, successful, independent development of Sikhism itself shows that Nanak was much more than just another teacher in this dissenting tradition of medieval Hinduism, called *nirgun bhakti* (devotion to the Formless).

Nanak's hymns combine a remarkable beauty and power of poetic expression with a distinctive coherence and ability for

Gurudwara Bangla Sahib, the most prominent Sikh gurdwara in Delhi, associated with the eighth Guru, Har Krishan, was first built in 1783.

systematic exposition, which is perhaps to be related to his professional background. Their contents embrace repeated praise of the divine order presided over and permeated by its creator, the one and only Immortal Being (*Akal Purakh*), with a penetrating analysis of the human condition, which is condemned through egotistical self-will (*haumai*, literally 'I-me') to the mechanical succession of suffering, and endless rebirths in blind unawareness of that order. In place of the false claims to offer true guidance offered by the religious specialists of the day, whether Brahmans, yogis, or Muslim clerics, Nanak sets out his own prescription for human salvation: the necessity of inner transformation through listening to the voice of the True Guru within the heart, and meditating with love upon the Divine Name. Only thus may freedom from self be gained, and escape from the cycle of transmigration be achieved, so that the liberated soul may at last join the company of saints in their eternal singing of praises at the court of the Immortal Being.

There is, however, nothing automatic about access to the path of salvation that Nanak describes. His hymns repeatedly emphasize that a righteous life is no guarantee of salvation, since the coming of the inner True Guru to any given individual depends on the favour of the Immortal Being. For this to happen, it is equally a necessary condition that the individual should have prepared him or herself for the True Guru's coming by living properly. Such a life does not entail the practice of elaborate rituals, or extreme asceticism, which are both frequently stated to be quite pointless. What is important is rather the discipline of living a normal life in this world, practising loving meditation on the divine reality, and supporting others through an honest existence, as summed up in the triple formula of 'the Name, giving, and keeping clean' (*nam dan isnan*).

THE LATER GURUS

As has been repeatedly demonstrated, the successful establishment of a religion depends not just upon the teachings of its founder, but also upon how the community created by them is subsequently organized. Besides being a teacher of outstanding force and insight, Guru Nanak was evidently a most capable organizer of his followers. He laid the foundations of some of the defining practices of the subsequent Sikh tradition, notably the establishment of daily offices of prayer (*nitnem*) and the practice of congregational assembly to hear the hymns of the Guru. Although married with two sons, Guru Nanak went outside his family to select a disciple to succeed him as the second Guru of the Sikh community, or *Panth* (path, way).

From the time of Guru Nanak's death, the Sikh Panth was led by a line of living Gurus, until the death of the tenth Guru in 1708. While rejection of the Hindu caste hierarchy was symbolically reinforced by the third Guru, Amar Das – through the institution of the *langar*, the temple kitchen offering food to all irrespective of caste – all the Gurus were from the same Khatri caste as Nanak; and from the fifth Guru onwards the succession became hereditary within a single family. Initially the centre of the community shifted with each Guru, until Guru Arjan founded the great temple at Amritsar known as the Golden Temple (*Harimandir*), which since its inauguration in 1604 has been the focal point of Sikhism.

At the same time, Guru Arjan undertook a project of still greater importance, in providing a unifying object of devotion for the Sikh Panth, through his codification of the Sikh scriptures, issued with the Guru's authority as the *Adi Granth* (original book). This is an enormous hymnal, filling 1,430 pages in the standard modern edition, and having a central place in the ritual of the Sikh temples, or *gurdwara* (gate of the Guru). Besides the compositions of Guru Nanak, the *Adi Granth* also contains those of the next four Gurus – who each used the same poetic name 'Nanak', in keeping with the belief that the transmission of the

THE TEN GURUS

Guru Nanak (1469–1539)
founder of Sikhism
Guru Angad (1539–52)
Guru Amar Das (1552–74)
Guru Ram Das (1574–81)
Guru Arjan (1581–1606)
Guru Hargobind (1606–44)
Guru Har Rai (1644–61)
Guru Har Krishan (1661–64)
Guru Tegh Bahadur (1664–75)
Guru Gobind Singh (1675–1708)

A BRIEF INTRODUCTION TO JAINISM AND SIKHISM

SIKHISM TIMELINE

1500 CE	1550 CE	1600 CE	1650 CE	1700 CE	1750 CE	1800 CE	1850 CE	1900 CE	1950 CE	2000 CE

1499 Nanak's mystical commissioning experience

1519 Nanak founds first Sikh community at Kartarpur

1539 Nanak succeeded by Angad

1577 Ram Das, fourth Guru, establishes town that becomes Amritsar

1603–4 Arjan, fifth Guru, sponsors compilation of Adi Granth

1606 Arjan martyred

1675 Tegh Bahadur, ninth Guru, martyred

1699 Gobind Singh, tenth Guru, organizes the Khalsa

1708 Succession of Gurus ends with death of Gobind Singh

1799 Punjab united under Maharaja Ramjit Singh

1873 Organization of the Singh Sabha movement ◆

1905 Hindu images removed from Golden Temple precincts in Amritsar ◆

1947 Partition of the Punjab between Pakistan and India ◆

1984 Indian government expels militants from the Golden Temple, killing hundreds of Sikhs ◆

THE *KHALSA*

On *Baisakhi* day in 1699, the tenth Guru founded the *Khalsa*, the community of initiated (*amritdhari*) Sikhs. The nucleus of this dynamic community is popularly known as the five beloved ones (*panj-piare*), who volunteered their readiness to sacrifice their lives for the sake of the Guru on that historic day.

Thereupon the Guru prepared *amrit* ('water of immortality') – popularly known as *khande di pahul* ('water of the double-edged sword') – for the initiation ceremony. The five volunteers, who belonged to different caste groups, drank *amrit* from the same bowl, signifying their entry into the casteless fraternity of the *Khalsa*. The next most important innovation was to change their names. All five volunteers, like the Guru, had traditional Hindu names before the initiation ceremony. Now they were given a new corporate name: 'Singh'. Afterwards, the Guru received *amrit* from the *panj-piare,* and changed his name from Gobind Rai to Gobind Singh. He also admitted women into the *Khalsa*, who after the initiation received the name 'Kaur'.

According to tradition, Guru Gobind Singh prescribed a new code of discipline for members of the *Khalsa*, which includes the wearing of five emblems, collectively known as *panj kakke* (five ks), because each begins with the letter '*kakka*' of the Gurmukhi script:

kes – uncut hair
kangha – a small wooden comb worn in hair
kirpan – a sword, nowadays a small one
kacha – a pair of knee-length breeches
kara – a steel bracelet worn on the right wrist

It is believed Gobind Singh also declared that members of the *Khalsa* must not smoke or chew tobacco, or consume alcohol. They should not eat meat slaughtered according to Muslim custom, and must not molest a Muslim woman. Although a turban (*pag*) is not one of the prescribed emblems, it has far greater significance for Sikhs than any other head-covering. A male Sikh is required to wear the turban in public as a symbol of commitment to Sikh ideals.

light of the guruship blended them into a seamless line of 'light blended into light' (*joti jot samai*). Guru Arjan himself is the largest single contributor, accounting for about one third of the whole. Its contents also include hymns by non-Sikh authors, such as Kabir and Ravidas, and the Muslim Farid, collectively referred to as 'devotees' (*bhagats*). The language of most of the scripture is a mixture of Old Punjabi and Old Hindi, written in the special Sikh script, *Gurmukhi.* The elaborate arrangement of several thousand hymns, itself an outstanding achievement of editorship, is not primarily by author, but by the mode (*raga*) in which they are to be sung. While no other early Sikh literature has the same canonical authority as the *Adi Granth*, popular devotion has always been fostered by the prose hagiographies of Guru Nanak – called *janamsakhis* (birth-witnesses) – which were first produced during this period.

GURU GOBIND SINGH AND THE *KHALSA*

The Panth grew significantly in numbers and membership during the time of the early Gurus, which overlapped the reign of the great Mughal emperor Akbar (1542–1605). But the strategic location of the Punjab inevitably embroiled the Gurus in imperial politics, and Guru Arjan became the first Sikh martyr, when Akbar's less tolerant successor ordered his execution. During the seventeenth century, the Panth expanded from its initial, largely professional and commercial, membership, to embrace increasing numbers of Sikhs from the Jat farming caste. At the same time, an increasingly militant policy was reflected in the proclamation under Arjan's son, Guru Hargobind, of claims to secular (*miri*) as well as spiritual authority (*piri*). Continuing conflict with the Mughals came to a further head with the execution in Delhi of the ninth Guru, Tegh Bahadur.

This led to a radical new formation of the community under the martyred leader's son, Guru Gobind Singh, the tenth and last Guru. Guru Gobind consciously adopted the role of a ruler, as well as that of guru, in his court at Anandpur, in the Punjab. His most important innovation was the re-establishment of the Guru's authority over the Panth, through the foundation of a new order called the *Khalsa*, the Guru's elite. While the Sikh Panth has always continued to contain many followers of Nanak and the gurus who choose not to become baptized members of the *Khalsa*, it is the latter who have led the Panth since the time of the last Guru. Gobind Singh's own sons were all killed in the course of his struggles against the forces of the Mughal emperor Aurangzeb (1618–1707), and he was himself killed by a Muslim assassin. After his death, the line of living Gurus came to an end, and their authority was henceforth vested in the scripture, expanded by the addition of Guru Tegh Bahadur's hymns to Guru Arjan's collection, and since revered as the *Guru Granth Sahib*.

> Surrounded, with no choice, in turn
> I too attacked with bow and gun.
> When matters pass all other means,
> It is allowed to take up arms.
>
> Dasam Granth 1391.

Compositions by Guru Gobind Singh, some of which form part of the daily liturgy, and many more by others associated with him, were assembled in another volume of lesser canonical status, the *Dasam Granth* (Book of the Tenth One). A further influential set of extra-canonical Sikh religious literature also came into being at around this time, in the form of the *Rahitnamas*, simple manuals prescribing various rules of conduct (*rahit*) for the Sikhs of the *Khalsa*.

During the eighteenth century, the Punjab was fought over between the declining Mughal Empire and new Muslim invaders from Afghanistan. This was the heroic age of the Sikh Panth, which was organized into local guerrilla bands, who mounted a spirited resistance to both sets of Muslim armies, and who even in defeat are remembered for their glorious acts of martyrdom (*shahidi*). Led and manned by the Jat Sikhs, who had now become the dominant group in the community, the *Khalsa* forces achieved complete political success with the capture of Lahore, the provincial capital, which became the centre of a powerful Sikh kingdom under Maharaja Ranjit Singh (1799–1839), whose generous patronage is responsible for the splendid appearance of many of the great Sikh temples today. But Ranjit Singh's weaker successors proved unable to resist the pressure of the British, who, after two hard-fought wars, finally incorporated the Punjab into their Indian Empire in 1849.

CHRISTOPHER SHACKLE

CHAPTER 16

Sacred Writings

Sikh scripture emerged under the leadership of human Gurus, and culminated in having ultimate authority within the Sikh tradition.

SRI GURU GRANTH SAHIB

The principal scripture of the Sikhs is the *Adi Granth*, the eternal book, or original collection of compositions in book form. In everyday Sikh usage, the *Adi Granth* is reverentially referred to as the *Sri Guru Granth Sahib*, which implies affirmation of faith in the scripture as Guru. The words *Sri* (Sir) and *Sahib* (Lord) are honorific titles, indicating the highest authority accorded to the scripture. The *Adi Granth* opens with the basic creed (*Mul Mantra*), affirming the fundamentals of the Sikh faith. It begins with the phrase 'Ek Onkar' (one God), signifying the oneness and unity of God, and affirms that the Supreme Being, or God, is 'One without a second'.

The *Adi Granth* was compiled by the fifth Guru, Arjan, in 1604, and contains the compositions of the first five Sikh Gurus, alongside the writings of Muslim and Hindu saints of the medieval period, some of whom belonged to the lowest caste group (*Shudra*). The entire collection is recorded in *Gurmukhi* script, which is also used for modern Punjabi. Because of its association with the Gurus and the scripture, *Gurmukhi* acquired a sacred status within the Sikh community.

The contents of the *Adi Granth* are respectfully referred to as *bani* (voice) and as *gurbani* (utterance of the Guru). Guru Nanak affirms the divine origin of the *bani*: 'As the *bani* of the Lord comes to me so do I proclaim its knowledge' (*Adi Granth* 722). The Guru is, in a primary sense, the 'voice' of God. Guru Nanak clarifies the distinction between the Divine Guru and the human Guru: he regarded himself as the minstrel (*dhadi*) of God (*Akal Purakh*), who openly proclaimed the glory of the divine Word (*Shabad*).

The process of identification of the *bani* with the Guru (God) began with Guru Nanak and was extended by his successors. For example, the third Guru, Amar Das, proclaimed: 'Love the *bani* of the Guru. It is our support in all places and it is bestowed by the Creator himself' (*Adi Granth* 1335). Similarly, the fourth Guru, Ram Das, says: 'The *bani* is the Guru, and the Guru the *bani*, and the nectar (*amrit*) permeates all souls …' (*Adi Granth* 982). The scripture concludes with Guru Arjan's hymn *Mundavani* (seal) which summarizes the essence of Sikh faith: 'In the platter are placed three things, truth, contentment, and wisdom, as well as the nectar of the Lord's Name [amrit-nam], the support of all.'

The *Adi Granth*, on its completion, was accorded the utmost sacred and authoritative status in 1604 when it was installed by Guru Arjan in the newly built Golden Temple (*Harimandir*) at Amritsar. Guru Arjan says: 'The book [*Adi Granth*] is the abode of the Supreme Lord.' From the time of Guru Nanak, the Sikh community began to use the *gurbani* in devotional singing (*shabad kirtan*) as part of congregational worship. Currently the original copy of the *Adi Granth* is in the possession of the Sodhi family at Kartarpur, Punjab.

The tenth Guru, Gobind Singh, terminated the line of human Gurus by bestowing guruship on the *Adi Granth*, to which he had added the compositions of his father, the ninth Guru, Tegh Bahadur. Since then, the *Adi Granth* has been revered as a human Guru, and is respectfully addressed as the *Sri Guru Granth Sahib*. It is placed on a high platform, under a canopy, and a ritual fan (*chauri*) is waved over it while a service is in progress. The presence of the *Guru Granth Sahib* is regarded as mandatory on almost all ceremonial and domestic occasions, such as weddings, initiation ceremonies, and naming ceremonies.

The *Dasam Granth* is the second scriptural book of the Sikhs, containing the compositions of the tenth Guru, Gobind Singh, and other poets, collected by Mani Singh after the death of Gobind Singh, and completed in 1734. The *Dasam Granth* is not installed in all *gurdwaras*, but is found at the two historic *gurdwaras* of Hazoor Sahib and Patna Sahib, popularly called *Takhat* (Throne of the Immortal Being), two of the five centres of temporal authority in Sikh society. Some of its compositions are recited during the preparation of *amrit* (water used for the initiation ceremony) and other acts of worship.

Bhai Gurdas was the scribe who wrote out the *Adi Granth*, under the direction of Guru Arjan. The collection of his writings is called *varan* (ballads), popularly known as 'the key to the *Adi Granth*', and normally sung and quoted by Sikh musicians and preachers at the *gurdwaras*.

SEWA SINGH KALSI

Guru Nanak on the Divine Name

If I could live for millions and millions of years, and if the air was my food and drink,

if I lived in a cave and never saw either the sun or the moon, and if I never slept, even in dreams

– even so, I could not estimate Your Value. How can I describe the Greatness of Your Name?

The True Lord, the Formless One, is Himself in His Own Place.

I have heard, over and over again, and so I tell the tale; as it pleases You, Lord, please instill within me the yearning for You.

If I was slashed and cut into pieces, and put into the mill and ground into flour,

burnt by all-consuming fire and mixed with ashes

– even then, I could not estimate Your Value. How can I describe the Greatness of Your Name?

If I was a bird, soaring and flying through hundreds of heavens,

and if I was invisible, neither eating nor drinking anything

– even so, I could not estimate Your Value. How can I describe the Greatness of Your Name?

Siri Ragu 2, Adi Granth 14–15.

CHAPTER 17

Beliefs

The central teaching in Sikhism is belief in the oneness of God: Sikh scripture begins with the phrase '*Ek Onkar*' (one God). All people – irrespective of caste, creed, colour, and sex – emanated from one divine source. Sikh Gurus have used a number of terms from Islamic and Hindu traditions for God, including Allah, Qadir, Karim, and Paar Brahma.

The diversity in God's creation is perceived as a divine gift, with all religious traditions regarded as capable of enriching the spiritual and cultural lives of their believers. According to Sikh teaching, all human groups evolved and developed their modes of worship and religious institutions within the context of their social environment. Reflecting on the essence and universality of religious truth, the tenth Guru, Gobind Singh, wrote:

Recognize all humankind, whether Muslim or Hindu as one. The same God is the Creator and Nourisher of all. Recognize no distinction among them. The temple and the mosque are the same. So are Hindu worship and Muslim prayer. Human beings are all one.

(Dasam Granth)

The nature of God is clearly manifested in Guru Nanak's first composition, the basic creed popularly known as the *Mul Mantra*, and in his first utterance, 'There is no Hindu, there is no Muslim.' The opening phrase of the *Mul Mantra* summarizes the fundamental belief of the Sikhs: the words '*Ek*' (one) and '*Onkar*' (God) emphasize the oneness of God. God is also believed to be the creator, from whom the universe has emanated. God is beyond the qualities of male and female; they are attributes of the creation, not the creator. Nanak says: 'The wise and beauteous Being is neither a man nor a woman nor a bird' (*Adi Granth* 1010).

Firstly God created light and then by his omnipotence, made all human beings. If we emanate from the same divine light, how can we say some are born higher than others? O, men, my brethren, stray ye not in doubt. Creation is in the Creator and the Creator is in Creation. He is fully filling all places.

Adi Granth 1349–50

As God is believed to be *ajuni*, he/she does not experience birth or die. God's having no gender further signifies the unity and equality of humankind.

Sikhism is strictly monotheistic: belief in God's incarnation and worship of idols is strongly disapproved of. Since God is without any form, colour, mark, or lineage, he/she cannot be installed as an idol. God is regarded as eternal truth (*ad sach*), without beginning and end, whereas everything else in this universe – including the sun, moon, stars, and earth – will perish. The notion of permanence applies only to God, who will remain divine truth forever.

HUKAM (DIVINE ORDER)

The term *hukam* (order, command) entered the Sikh/Punjabi vocabulary from Arabic. In Islam, God is perceived as one who gives orders, a commander (*Hakam*). In Sikhism, *hukam* is perceived as the divine order; everything in this universe is believed to be working according to God's *hukam*. The Sikh gurus used the concept of *hukam* extensively in their compositions to describe the nature of creation, the universe, and human life. Nanak refers to *hukam* as the divine hand behind the functioning of the universe, as well as behind the daily lives of human beings.

Although human beings are unique in God's creation, alone endowed with the ability to discriminate between good and evil, the most significant aspects of human existence, such as birth and death, are beyond their control. Human life (*manas janam*) is a divine gift; both birth and death occur according to *hukam*. At Sikh funerals, death is explained as eternal reality; it occurs according to the *Alahi Hukam* (divine order, Allah's order). Therefore, mortals must submit to God's will, without any doubt or questioning. Guru Nanak reflects on the concept of *hukam* by posing the question, 'How may a man purify himself? ... This is brought about by living in accordance with God's command or will' (*Hukam Adi Granth 2*).

The concept of *hukam* raises a fundamental question. Are mortals helpless creatures in God's kingdom? Sikh teachings reject this view, and proclaim that all human beings are endowed with the ability to determine their own destiny. If someone commits evil deeds, he or she will suffer accordingly: that which one sows, that one shall reap. Ultimately, falsehood and evil will be destroyed, and truth prevail. For the attainment of truth, one needs to engage in righteous deeds.

MUKTI (SPIRITUAL LIBERATION)

The word *mukti* is the Punjabi version of the Sanskrit term *moksha* (to be free from, to release), denoting the final release, or spiritual liberation, of the soul from human existence, leading to merging with the Supreme Soul (*Parmatma*). According to the Sikh teaching, the soul (*atma*) is immortal, while the body in which it resides is perishable. After death, the body is cremated, and the *atma* either merges with the Supreme Soul, or passes from one form of life to another, depending upon one's *karma* in this world. As a religious concept, the term *karma* (literally: deeds, actions) denotes one's preordained destiny. Although Sikhs believe in the doctrine of *karma*, they do not regard human beings as helpless creatures. The notion of *jivan-mukta* (see below) transcends the limitations of *karma*, and transforms it into a dynamic force.

For the cycle of birth and death, the Sikh Gurus used the term *awagaun*, based on the doctrine of *karma* and the transmigration of souls. According to traditional Hindu belief, there are 8,400,000 forms of existence before one is reborn as a human being. Those who are sinful, and engage in evil-doing, keep going through the cycle of birth and death regarded as the most degrading state: *narak* (hell). At a Sikh funeral, the officiant recites the final prayer (*antam-ardas*) invoking God's forgiveness for the departed soul, and saving him or her from *awagaun*.

To avoid the ultimate punishment of *chaurasi* (cycle of birth and death), Sikhs are required to conduct themselves according to the teachings of the Sikh Gurus, working towards becoming Guru-oriented (*gursikh*), rather than self-oriented (*manmukh*). A Sikh is taught to live as an honest householder, a true believer in the oneness of God and the equality of humankind, while earning a living by honest means (*kirat karna*), and sharing with others (*vand chhakna*).

A Sikh who succeeds in attaining the status of *gursikh* is called *jivan-mukta*, liberated from worldly temptations such as lust (*kaam*), anger (*krodh*), greed (*lobh*), attachment (*moh*), and false pride or ego (*ahankar*). Another attribute of a *jivan-mukta* is his or her faith in *gurbani* to earn *mukti* now rather than after death. A *gursikh* transforms into a *jivan-mukta* by leading a life of detachment from worldly temptations, while actively engaged in the social and cultural enrichment of society, or *seva* (voluntary service). A *jivan-mukta* Sikh is like a lotus that remains clean, despite living in muddy water.

DHARMSAL (PRACTICE OF RIGHTEOUSNESS)

The term *dharmsal* is composed of *dharm* (religious, moral, and social obligations) and *sal* (a place of abode). Guru Nanak describes the earth as *dharmsal* (a place to practise righteousness), established by God within the universe. In this *dharmsal*, human life is regarded as the highest and most precious form, as well as a divine gift. The earth, and everything in it, is believed to carry the divine stamp.

> *In pride, man is overtaken by fear. In utter commotion he passes his life. Pride is a great malady because of which, he dies, is reborn and continues coming and going.*
>
> Adi Granth 592

According to Sikh teaching, Sikhs are not passive spectators, or recluses, in this world; they are expected to be active participants in human affairs, and Guru-oriented (*gursikh*). The concept of *dharmsal* implies faith in the oneness of God, and in the equality of humankind. Guru Nanak reprimanded Hindu ascetics (*yogis*) who advocated the path of renunciation, abdicating their social obligations. Apart from Har Krishan, who died aged eight, all the Sikh gurus were married men, who demonstrated their faith in their adherence to the householder's state (*grihsth-ashrama-dharma*). For a Sikh, there is no place for the renunciation of society.

GURPARSAD (GRACE AND BLESSING)

The term *gurparsad* is composed of *gur* (from *guru*) and *parsad* (Sanskrit for grace, blessing), which is also applied to the sanctified food offered to the congregation at the culmination of a Sikh service. *Gurparsad* is the last word of the *Mul Mantra*, standing for the eternal Guru (God), and affirms Sikh belief, and the way God can be realized. The Sikh Gurus used several terms to elaborate the concept of *gurparsad*, such as *karam* (Arabic), *mehar* and *nadar* (Persian), and *kirpa* (Sanskrit). It is believed that everyone's destiny is preordained, according to his or her *karma*, and ultimately one is responsible for its consequences. Guru Nanak says, 'Through grace is reached the Door of The Divine' (*Adi Granth* 145), and that, as one spark of fire can burn huge amounts of firewood, so acts of devotion and love of God may annul the consequences of bad *karma*. The Sikh Gurus repeatedly affirm that divine grace is the fruit of sincere devotion to God.

Two elderly Sikhs at the Gurudwara Bangla Sahib, Delhi. Note their long turbans and distinctive metal bangles.

NAMSIMRAN (MEDITATING ON GOD'S NAME)

The concept of *nam* (name) is one of the key doctrines in Sikhism, symbolizing the eternal truth, or God. In everyday usage, the term *namsimran* is applied to the discipline of daily meditation undertaken by devout Sikhs, during which it is common practice to use a rosary, often repeating the words *Waheyguru* and *Satnam*. Many Sikhs participate in *namsimran* sessions organized at *gurdwaras*.

The Sikh Gurus used the concept of *nam* to affirm their faith in the omnipresence of God, and impressed upon their disciples the necessity of the discipline of *namsimran*. They assert that *nam* is the creator of everything; through nam comes all wisdom and light; *nam* extends to all creation; there is no place where *nam* is not.

SEWA SINGH KALSI

CHAPTER 18

Worship and Festivals

In popular Sikh usage, the act of worship means reading from the scripture and reciting a selection of hymns (*path-karna*). In individual or congregational worship the central focus is on the utterances of the Gurus in the *Adi Granth* (*gurbani*). Sikh festivals, which are both religious and cultural celebrations, fall into two categories: *gurpurb*, an anniversary when a Guru is remembered, and *mela*, a fair. The most popular melas are *Baisakhi*, *Diwali*, and *Hola*.

INDIVIDUAL WORSHIP

The pattern of individual worship is prescribed in the Sikh code of discipline (*Rehat Maryada*), published in 1951. The daily routine (*nitnem*) comprises texts from the *Adi Granth* and rules for personal cleanliness. A Sikh should rise early and take a bath, then recite the hymns of *Japji*, *Jap*, and *Ten Sawayyas*. At sunset he or she should recite the hymn of *Rahiras*, and before going to bed recite the hymn of *Sohila* and the prayer *ardas* (petition).

Worship can be undertaken anywhere in peace and quiet, and most Sikh households have a collection of hymns normally recited during worship (*gutka*), wrapped in cloth and kept in a safe place. Many devout Sikhs also have a copy of the *Guru Granth Sahib* at home, respectfully kept in a special room, usually located on the top floor. Although any building where a copy of the *Guru Granth Sahib* is installed qualifies to be called a *gurdwara*, a family *gurdwara* is strictly a private shrine, not open to the general public.

CONGREGATIONAL WORSHIP

Congregational worship takes place at the *gurdwara*. There is no fixed day, but in the diaspora most services take place on a Sunday. The term *gurdwara* is composed of *guru* (denoting the *Guru Granth Sahib*) and *dwara* (gate or house), and is attributed to the sixth Guru, Hargobind, who is believed to have built *gurdwaras* at sites associated with his predecessors. During the period of the first five Gurus, a Sikh place of worship was known as a *dharmsala*. According to tradition, Guru Nanak established the first at Kartarpur, as a place where a congregation (*sangat*) of men and women of all caste groups would gather for communal worship and hymn-singing (*shabad kirtan*), followed by a communal meal (*langar*). The institutions of *sangat*, *shabad kirtan*, and *langar* emerged as distinguishing features of the Sikh tradition.

Historic *gurdwaras* have been built on sites linked to important events in the development of Sikhism: for example, Gurdwara Kesgarh at Anandpur, where the tenth Guru, Gobind Singh, established the *Khalsa* in 1699; and Gurdwara Sis Ganj in Delhi, built where the ninth Guru, Tegh Bahadur, was beheaded by the Mughal authorities. Community-based *gurdwaras* are autonomous institutions, established by local Sikh communities, and run by locally elected management committees, which are answerable only to their local *sangat*.

A similar pattern of service is observed at all *gurdwaras*, beginning with the recital and singing of *Asa di var* in the morning, followed by more hymn-singing from scripture. The service concludes with the recital of *ardas* by the *granthi* (reader of the scripture), while members of the *sangat* stand silently with folded hands. After the *ardas*, a randomly chosen hymn from the scripture is read out to the congregation, called *hukam-nama* (divine order for the day). The service ends with the distribution of sanctified food (*karah parshad*) to members of the congregation, symbolizing Sikh belief in the equality of humankind.

The way a Sikh expresses his or her reverence for the scripture might create the impression that the Sikhs are idol worshippers: for example, when a Sikh enters the congregational hall, he or she approaches the *Adi Granth*, makes an offering, and bows. In fact, the devotee is showing devotion towards the teachings of the Gurus, *Guru Granth Sahib*.

GURPURBS

The term *gurpurb* is made up of *gu* (short for *guru*) and *purb* (a sacred or auspicious day). Four main *gurpurbs* are celebrated by Sikhs throughout the world:
- The birthday of Guru Nanak: 26 November
- The birthday of Guru Gobind Singh: 5 January
- The martyrdom anniversary of Guru Arjan: 16 June
- The martyrdom anniversary of Guru Tegh Bahadur: 24 November

In India, *gurpurbs* are celebrated by carrying the *Guru Granth Sahib* in processions around towns and villages. In villages, the scripture is placed in a decorated palanquin (*palki*), and the procession is led by five initiated (*amritdhari*) Sikhs carrying swords, symbolizing the 'five beloved ones' initiated by the tenth Guru in 1699.

THE GOLDEN TEMPLE

The Golden Temple (*Harimandir*) at Amritsar, India, serves as a symbol of the Sikh religion, and as a visual aid to our understanding of its spiritual meaning, and how the past has influenced the present. For Sikhs this temple is the court of the Lord (*Dharbar Sahib*), and in its precincts are found peace and the possibility of access to God.

The Hindi and Punjabi hymns of the early Gurus, together with those of some non-Sikh mystics, were collected together and first installed here by Arjan in 1604. Later editions of this volume, which include the devotional poetry of the later Gurus, constitute the focal point of devotion and meditation. The hymns are sung from morning to night at the temple, and a constant stream of visitors and pilgrims comes to listen to the words, which confer a blessing on believing hearers.

The temple site consists of an outer paved area, with shaded cloisters surrounding the large pool, or tank, from which Amritsar ('pool of nectar') takes its name. At the centre of the pool stands the beautiful Golden Temple itself, in which the sacred book is placed early in the morning.

This temple has served as the basis for many interpretations of the religious life. It is, for example, like a lotus plant growing from the murky water of life,

producing a beautiful flower of devotion and good works – teaching people to reach above the evil of the world, which would choke their higher desires. The outer courtyard possesses four entrances, unlike the single doorways of Muslim and Hindu shrines, expressing the universality of Sikh truth, which is open to all.

Another gold-topped building stands in the outer area, facing the long walkway to the inner holy place. This is the *Akal Takhat*, a political and community centre, where important pronouncements are made concerning the life of Sikhs. Built by the sixth Guru, it indicates the rise of political and social awareness among Sikhs, as they sought to establish a code of conduct for themselves, and a way of organizing their relations with other groups. Here, in the temple area, religion and politics are clearly distinguished.

There are four other major *Takhats* (or thrones), and many other important temples; but Amritsar provides a clear demonstration of the great unity of social and religious life which has emerged in Sikh culture.

Douglas Davies

The Golden Temple, or Harmandir Sahib, Amritsar, Punjab, India.

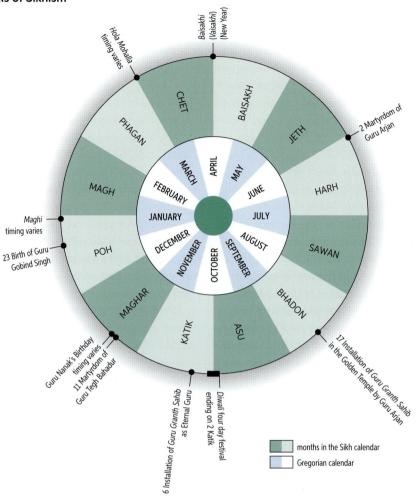

BAISAKHI

The festival of *Baisakhi* is celebrated on the first day of the month of *Baisakh* in the Punjabi calendar, and nowadays has a special importance for the Sikhs as it marks the birthday of the *Khalsa*. In Punjab, farmers begin harvesting the wheat crop after the *Baisakhi* celebrations. Apart from religious ceremonies, a number of cultural activities are organized, such as *kabadi*, football, hockey, and wrestling. Traditional *Bhangra* dancing, when dancers dress up in colourful Punjabi costumes, is the climax of the celebrations.

HOLA

Hola takes its name from the traditional Hindu festival of *Holi*, which is celebrated by communal singing, dancing, and throwing colours on people, irrespective of caste, gender, and status. Guru Gobind Singh disapproved of the *Holi* festival, regarding it as wasteful and degrading. He summoned his followers to Anandpur to celebrate the festival of *Holi* differently: instead of merrymaking, he organized mock battles between two groups of Sikh volunteers, and trained them in martial arts, thereby giving them a new purpose in life. The title of the festival was changed to *Hola*, and the tradition of martial arts remains associated with it.

DIWALI

Diwali is one of the traditional festivals of India, popularly known as the festival of lights; its origin is traced to the homecoming of Lord Rama from exile. Hindus illuminate their homes and temples, and exchange gifts of sweets with friends and relatives. The festival has another significance for Sikhs: it is associated with the release of the sixth Guru, Hargobind, from the Gwalior Fort, where he was imprisoned by the Mughal emperor Jahangir. The Guru's arrival in Amritsar was celebrated by the illumination of the city by his followers. Nowadays, special *Diwali* services are conducted at the *gurdwaras*, celebrating the release of Guru Hargobind, and affirming a distinct Sikh identity. *Gurdwaras* and private houses are decorated with candles, and firework displays are organized. The tradition of illuminating the Golden Temple (*Harimandir*) marks the climax of the *Diwali* festivities.

GURU HARGOBIND'S RELEASE

According to Sikh tradition, Guru Hargobind was imprisoned by the emperor Jahangir in the Gwalior Fort on the suspicion that he had raised a large army to fight against the government. 52 Hindu princes were already imprisoned in the fort. After several years, the authorities ordered the Guru's release, but he refused to go until the other princes were set free. The emperor agreed to the Guru's demand, and said he would release as many princes as could come out holding the Guru's garment and hands. On hearing this condition, the Guru ordered a special cloak, which had many strips of cloth, and in this way all 52 princes came out of the fort holding the Guru's garment and hands. Thus the Guru became popular as *Bandi Chhod* (deliverer of prisoners).

SANGRAND

The first day of every month in the Hindu lunar calendar is called *Sangrand*, from the Sanskrit word *sangkrant*, denoting the entrance of the sun into a new sign of the Zodiac. In Sikhism, it is observed in a special service (*diwan*) at the *gurdwara*, with the name of the new month ritually announced from scripture. Guru Arjan composed the 'hymn of twelve months'

(*Bara Maha*), each of its twelve parts illustrating a stage of life and the journey of the soul, while directing the Sikhs to conform to the prescribed code of discipline each month. Before setting off to work on this festival

Pool, or sarovar, at the Sikh Gurudwara Bangla Sahib, Delhi, India, whose water is considered holy.

day, Sikhs visit the *gurdwara* to invoke divine grace for the well-being of their family and the whole of humankind. Listening to the recital of the name of the new month is perceived as a meritorious boon. The festival of *Baisakhi* occurs at *Sangrand* in the month of *Baisakh* (usually 14 April) and the ceremony of replacing the old covering of the flagpole with a new one (*Nishan Sahib*) takes place at the *gurdwaras* on this day.

SEWA SINGH KALSI

CHAPTER 19

Family and Society

The Sikh movement emerged in the context of a caste-ridden Indian society, in which occupation and status were ascribed and determined on the basis of one's birth into a particular caste group (*Jaat*), and there was no significant social interaction between members of different caste groups. Sikh Gurus were acutely aware of the destructive impact of the caste system on the social, religious, and cultural fabric of Indian society, and rejected the Hindu doctrine of *varnashramadharma* — laws of social classes and stages of life — which they saw as based on caste exclusiveness and institutionalized inequality.

Although Sikh teachings reject the doctrine of caste, its influence is sometimes still seen within the Sikh community. The joint family, or the extended household, is the basic unit within Punjabi Sikh society, and has a traditional occupation, such as *Jaat* (farmer), *Tarkhan* (carpenter), or *Chamar* (leather-worker).

Several domestic rites provide insight into the interaction between religious and social customs, such as marriage, birth, and death.

MARRIAGE

Marriage is regarded as the bedrock of Sikh society; Sikhism rejects celibacy and renunciation. All Sikh Gurus, except Guru Har Krishan, who died at the age of eight, were married men. They strongly advocated that Sikhs should lead as householders (*grihasthi*), recognizing their duties to parents, wife, and children — and to the wider society.

> Worthless is caste and worthless an exalted name.
>
> For all mankind there is but only one refuge.'
>
> Guru Nanak, *Adi Granth* 83.

Sikh marriage is more than the simple unification of man and a woman; it is regarded as an alliance between two families. The scriptures consider marriage to be a spiritual bond, and emphasize the concept of one spirit in two bodies (*ek jote doye murti*). The fourth Guru, Ram Das, says: 'They are not man and wife who have physical contact only. Only they are truly wedded who have one spirit in two bodies' (*Adi Granth* 788). In addition, the marital relationship is perceived as a relationship preordained by God (*sanjog*), not a social contract. However, Sikhs are permitted to remarry if a marriage irretrievably breaks down.

THE MARRIAGE CEREMONIES

The engagement ceremony (*kurmai, mangni*) begins with the recital of a prayer (*ardas*). A special hymn of *kurmai* is recited from the *Adi Granth*, and a *hukamnama* is read out for God's blessing.

The customary meeting of the heads of both families (*milni*) begins with the recital of *ardas* by the *granthi*, who prays for God's blessing on the alliance of the two families. Then the bride's father formally greets the groom's father, and makes a gift of a turban, and sometimes money.

The guests attend the *gurdwara* for the wedding ceremony (*anand karaj*), where bride and groom sit in front of the *Adi Granth*. The most popular colour for brides to wear is red. The bride usually wears a *lengha* – tunic and long skirt – made of the same material, but some wear a sari or trouser suit (*salwar kamiz*). The bride does not wear a veil, but covers her head with a long scarf (*chuni*). The groom often wears a red or maroon turban.

The *anand karaj* begins with *ardas*, followed by the ritual joining of the couple with the groom's scarf (*palla pharana*) by the bride's father. At this stage the religious musicians (*ragis*) sing *palley taindey lagi*, a hymn from the *Adi Granth* which stresses the sanctity of the marital bond. There are four wedding hymns, collectively called *lavan*. After each, the couple walks around the *Adi Granth* in a clockwise direction, the bridegroom leading the bride. The *anand karaj* concludes with the recital of the hymn *anand sahib* and *ardas*.

A young Sikh in the Punjab.

CHILDREN

The birth of a child is regarded as a divine gift (*waheyguru di dat*). Traditionally, children were given names by their grandparents, or by their paternal aunt. Nowadays, most Sikh families visit the *gurdwara* and ask for an *akhar* – usually the first letter on the page where the *Adi Granth* is opened – and a name is chosen that begins with this letter. In addition, Sikh boys are given the title *Singh* (lion), and girls *Kaur* (princess).

The turban (*pag*) is a symbol of honour, but there is no stipulation of the age when a Sikh boy starts to wear it. Usually, he will be eleven or twelve, and thus able to look after it. The turban may be of any colour, and is normally of muslin and 15 feet (about five metres) long.

DEATH

In India, funerals usually take place very soon after death, or on the next day. The body is bathed and dressed in new clothes, before cremation. It is a son's duty to light the pyre; in the absence of a son, another male relative performs this rite. Before this, a *granthi* recites *ardas* for the departed soul. Women are prohibited from helping to carry the bier, or lighting the pyre. At the death of a married woman (*sohagan*), her shroud is provided by her paternal family, and she is dressed as a bride. In the Punjab, the ashes are collected after three days, and usually deposited in running water. After the funeral, the deceased's family organize the reading of the *Adi Granth*, either at their home or at the local *gurdwara*.

If the deceased was a man, the ritual of *pagri* – transfer of paternal authority – takes place at this time. This ceremony involves the chief mourner – the oldest son – who sits in front of the *Adi Granth* and receives a turban and some money from his maternal uncle. He wears the new turban in the presence of his relatives and members of the congregation, then a senior member of the *biradari* reminds him of his new status and responsibilities. The social function of *pagri* is to facilitate the incorporation of a son into the role of his father.

SEWA SINGH KALSI

I AM A SIKH

I was born in a Sikh village called Talhan, in the state of Punjab, India. It had its own large temple (*gurdwara*). Every year, the residents of the village and the surrounding areas celebrated the important religious festivals and took part in processions, and with the other children I joined in. My early nurturing in Sikh traditions took place within my family and this village community. I knew the basic beliefs of Sikhism at a very young age.

In 1968 my family moved to Leeds, England. I was only nine, and this was quite an experience for all of us. None of us could speak English. We found it hard to socialize, and everything around us felt very different. We were fortunate to have a very helpful English family next door. They had two daughters the same age as myself. We used to play together, and their father took me to school on my first day, because my parents could not speak English. This helped us settle in at our local primary school, and made us feel at home in Leeds. At school, we began to learn English. We were very keen and worked hard, attending extra English classes for Asian children. We made lots of friends. At that time there was only one *gurdwara* in Leeds – simply called 'the Sikh temple'. Although it was a three-mile walk from our house, we attended regularly on Sundays. I also attended Punjabi classes there.

Attending the *gurdwara* on a regular basis for prayers, in the presence of the congregation, and listening to hymn-singing (*shabad kirtan*), helped me understand the meaning of 'the oneness of God'. I began to take part in voluntary help (*seva*) in the community kitchen (*langar*). Food is served to everyone attending, including visitors from other faiths and backgrounds. Importantly, all are served the same meal, as this shows equality.

Soon after we arrived in Leeds, my elder brother and I had a haircut. In our new surroundings, we were embarrassed to have long hair. When I moved to secondary school, I met a young Sikh who wore a turban. I was impressed, and soon began to grow my hair again and wear a turban. Although I am not an 'initiated Sikh', I wear a turban to identify myself as a follower. I also wear a steel bracelet (*kara*) on my right wrist. My middle name is Singh, a name given to all male Sikhs by the tenth Guru. I do not cut my hair or trim my beard, and do not drink or smoke, both of which are against Sikh teachings.

My religious discipline is based on Sikh teachings, central to which is the belief that there is only one God. My daily commitments include meditation on God's name (*nam japna*), sharing with others (*vand chhakna*), voluntary service (*seva*), and earning my living honestly (*kirat karna*). These are most important for every Sikh. Every morning before breakfast I say the morning prayer, the *Mul Mantra*. My mother taught me this when I was young, and since she passed away – more than twenty years ago – I have said it daily. I regularly participate in religious activities and festivals at the *gurdwara*,

A BRIEF INTRODUCTION TO JAINISM AND SIKHISM

such as *Baisakhi, Diwali* and other celebrations. These bring the community and families together, enabling the younger generation, including my children, to learn more about Sikhism.

Gradually, my involvement at the *gurdwara* has increased, as has my commitment to helping others. As Sikhs, we take part in the activities of Leeds Concord multi-faith fellowship. Recently my youngest daughter lit the candles at the Peace Service, on behalf of the Sikh community. I regularly contribute towards Sikh activities, including donations towards the upkeep of the *gurdwara* and the community kitchen (*langar*). My job as a Technical Liaison Officer involves a lot of travelling. I come into contact with people of different backgrounds and faiths, and with my turban, beard and so on, I openly display my commitment to my faith. I enjoy my work and, as I do it, I apply my faith's teaching about equality and truthful living (*kirat karna*).

My wife came from India in 1983 and, having completed postgraduate studies, became a primary school teacher in Leeds. Because of my cultural tradition, I had an arranged marriage, conducted at the *gurdwara* in the presence of the Sikh holy book (*Guru Granth Sahib*) and the congregation. Verses from the *Guru Granth Sahib* were read out and sung by the priest. Not only did I marry a person of the same religion, but we also bring up our three children within the faith. Both my wife's and my own influence on the children has encouraged them to speak Punjabi as well as English, and to attend the *gurdwara* on a regular basis. I hope that, by learning the value of prayer, by understanding the importance of helping and respecting others, and by learning the Gurus' teachings, my children will follow me in the faith and commit their lives to God.

As a family, we have visited India. As well as seeing the tourist attractions, we visited many *gurdwaras* in the Punjab and Delhi. Our visit to the famous Golden Temple at Amritsar was most exciting, and gave me a greater understanding of my religious tradition.

I have enjoyed music from an early age, particularly *shabad kirtan*. I can listen to *shabad kirtan* in the morning before going to work, as well as in the evening. I find this very helpful in my quest to learn more about the Sikh faith. It is also helpful for my children. However, we don't listen to religious music alone. We also enjoy traditional Indian music, folk music, and *bhangra* dancing.

I think the teachings of the Sikh faith have made me a better person. I thank God, who has given me so much and, in return, I want to give back to God as much of myself as I can, by committing myself to the Sikh faith.

Resham Singh Bhogal

CHAPTER 20

Sikhism Today

The evolution of Sikhism has remained closely involved with political and social developments in the Punjab, throughout a century of British rule, and since 1947 in independent India. Like many other Asian religions, Sikhism first experienced the challenges of modernity at the same time as those of nineteenth-century European colonialism. A Sikh reform movement proved remarkably successful in articulating for much of the twentieth century a reinforced Sikhism, which survived the community's traumatic experience of the partition of Punjab between India and Pakistan in 1947. More recent decades, however, have been marked by tensions between the politicized expression of Sikhism, which grew out of the reform movement, and an Indian political leadership increasingly identified with Hindu majoritarianism. The same period also saw the establishment of substantial Sikh diasporas in Britain and North America, where the challenges of adapting Sikhism to the very different circumstances of the international, twenty-first century, English-speaking world are most acutely faced.

SIKH REFORM

In the heyday of colonial rule, in the later nineteenth century, the leaders of all sections of Indian society, including the Sikhs, had to confront the linked implications of British political dominance and their dominant Victorian world view, with its strongly Christian emphasis. A path of total resistance to modernity was chosen by a few, such as Baba Ram Singh (1816–84), but his self-proclamation as Guru confined his support to the Namdhari Sikh sect which he founded.

The mainstream leadership realized, however, that a more complex process of accommodation to the new order was required for the successful survival of the Sikh community. The Sikhs' distinct religious identity was seen to be doubly threatened: by the dismantling of state-supported Sikh political institutions after the British conquest of Ranjit Singh's kingdom, and by the threat of assimilation into a resurgent Hinduism. The latter threat was forcefully articulated in the Punjab by the modernist Arya Samaj organization, founded by Dayananda Sarasvati (1824–83), whose doctrine of all truth being found in the *Vedas* was found offensively dismissive of the teachings of the Sikh Gurus.

To combat these challenges, a number of reformist associations (*Singh Sabhas*) were founded in the main cities of the Punjab. Through these associations, and making full use of the new communication systems established by the colonial state, a number of gifted lay leaders, often honoured with the title *Bhai* (Brother), came to formulate a redefinition of Sikhism which has remained the dominant orthodoxy to the present day. Like most reformers, the *Singh Sabha* activists saw the contemporary plight of Sikhism as the consequence of a falling away from the pristine ideals of an earlier age. They diagnosed an increasing reversion to Hinduism in both religious and social practice as the cause of what had gone wrong, and preached the necessity of a return to the glorious age of the Gurus, marked by uncompromising monotheism, and the adoption of a simple and devout lifestyle untainted by superstition. The title of the most famous of many tracts through which their message was disseminated, 'We are not Hindus' (*Ham Hindu Nahin*, 1898), by Bhai Kahn Singh Nabha (1867–1938), points to the cornerstone of the reformists' programme, their strenuous efforts to distinguish the Sikhs of the *Khalsa* as a community quite separate from its Hindu origins and traditionally close ties with Hinduism.

The reformists often justified their definition of Sikhism in relation to Hinduism by an analogy of the relation betweens between Protestantism and Roman Catholicism. Fitting well with imperial policies of 'divide and rule', it found particular favour with the British, as a way of ensuring the separate loyalty of their Sikh troops, who were recruited as a reliable minority, out of all proportion to their numbers in the population – and army regulations specified strict adherence to *Khalsa* practice in the Sikh regiments. At the same time, a remarkable cultural transformation was effected within the Sikh community itself, through the literary and scholarly activity of leading reformers such as Bhai Vir Singh (1872–1957). Developing Punjabi in the Gurmukhi script as a vehicle for modern communication, they produced new editions of the scriptures with extensive commentaries, and an impressive body of creative writing, which often drew upon the mythic power of Sikh history to drive home the reformist message.

SIKH POLITICAL ACTIVISM

By the end of World War I, the reformists had given the Sikhs the confidence and coherence to engage with the nationalist politics of the late colonial period. A new activist phase was launched with the *Akali* movement, established to push through the transfer of control of the major *gurdwaras* from their hereditary guardians, who administered their vast endowments, often for private profit. A programme of mass demonstrations, producing violent conflicts and fresh martyrs for the cause, eventually resulted in government sanction for the Sikh *Gurdwaras* Act of 1925, which gave control of the great *gurdwaras* of the Punjab to an elected committee of male Sikhs, the Shiromani Gurdwara Prabandhak Committee (SGPC), which became the single most important voice within Sikhism, and through its resources now supports the *Akali Dal*, the main Sikh political party. The British refused Sikh women the right to become members; however, since Indian independence in 1947, women have been elected, even to the prestigious post of secretary and president.

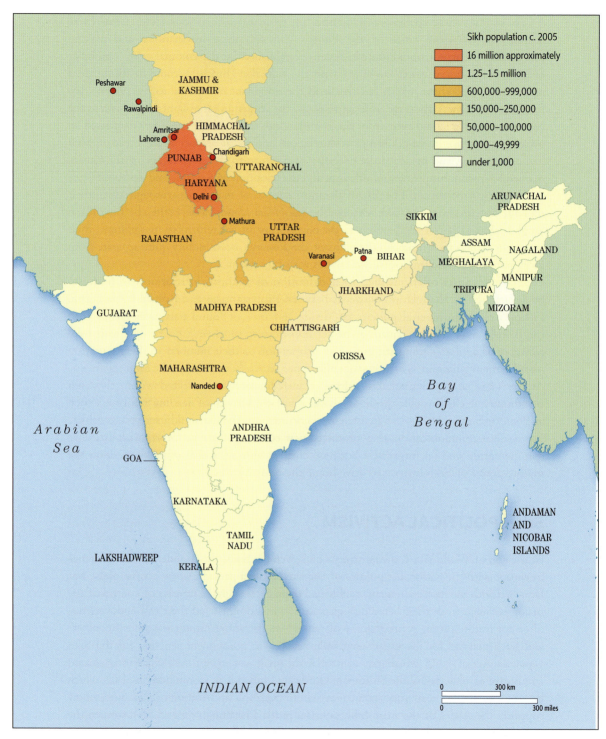

Sikh population c. 2005

▮	16 million approximately
▮	1.25–1.5 million
▮	600,000–999,000
▮	150,000–250,000
▮	50,000–100,000
▮	1,000–49,999
▮	under 1,000

Peshawar
Rawalpindi
JAMMU & KASHMIR
HIMMACHAL PRADESH
Amritsar
Lahore
Chandigarh
PUNJAB
UTTARANCHAL
HARYANA
Delhi
ARUNACHAL PRADESH
Mathura
SIKKIM
RAJASTHAN
UTTAR PRADESH
ASSAM
NAGALAND
MEGHALAYA
Varanasi
Patna BIHAR
MANIPUR
JHARKHAND
TRIPURA
GUJARAT
MADHYA PRADESH
MIZORAM
CHHATTISGARH
ORISSA
MAHARASHTRA
Nanded
Bay of Bengal
Arabian Sea
ANDHRA PRADESH
GOA
ANDAMAN AND NICOBAR ISLANDS
KARNATAKA
TAMIL NADU
LAKSHADWEEP
KERALA
INDIAN OCEAN

0   300 km
0   300 miles

Sikhism in India Today

A BRIEF INTRODUCTION TO JAINISM AND SIKHISM

For the next decades, the leaders' chief energies were devoted to the pursuit of a political settlement that would guarantee the position of Sikhs as a distinctive ethno-religious minority. The approach of Indian independence was marked by increasing polarization between Hindus and Muslims. With no realistic chance of achieving their own country, the Sikhs' lot was cast with the Hindus in 1947, when the partition of the Punjab between India and Pakistan was effected, at the cost of massive ethnic cleansing. Although this uprooted half the community that found itself on the Pakistan side, its resettlement in Indian Punjab in place of the departed Muslim population had the effect of consolidating the Sikh population territorially for the first time.

Young Sikhs at a national gathering in Italy, 2011.

From this base, and building on Sikh identification with Punjabi, the *Akali Dal* launched the *Punjabi Suba*, or Punjabi State campaign, with the aim of establishing within the Indian Union a linguistically-defined state with a Punjabi-speaking – that is, Sikh – majority. Although this was achieved with the separation of a truncated Sikh-dominated Punjab from the Hindu-majority state of Haryana in 1966, this did not halt the dangerous religio-political momentum that had been set in motion. By the early 1980s, the Punjab became a battleground, with armed Sikh activists, inspired by the ideal of establishing Khalistan as an independent Sikh country, opposed by the Indian security forces. This culminated in the notorious events of 1984 at Amritsar, when the Indian prime minister, Indira Gandhi (1917–84), ordered the army to storm the *Harimandir* – which had been occupied by the followers of the charismatic young preacher Sant Jarnail Singh Bhindranvale (1947–84). Her own later assassination by her Sikh bodyguards provoked anti-Sikh pogroms in many parts of India, killing thousands. The separatist cause eventually lost the support of most Sikhs in India.

ORGANIZATION AND AUTHORITY

The rules of reformed Sikhism are set out in the official *Guide to the Sikh Way of Life* (*Rehat Maryada*), first issued as a pamphlet by the SGPC in 1945. It defines a Sikh as any person

*   whose faith is in one God, the ten Gurus and their teaching, and the *Adi Granth*
*   believes in the necessity and importance of initiation (*amrit*)
*   does not adhere to any other religion.

Sikhism is a religion without priests, so authority in the larger *gurdwaras* rests with the lay committees which run them, not with the 'keepers of the scripture' (*granthis*) whom they employ.

THE SIKH DIASPORAS

The necessarily rather rigid redefinitions of Sikhism first formulated by the *Singh Sabha* leaders in the late nineteenth century are beginning to be perceived as in need of adjustment, to meet the changed circumstances of the twenty-first century. With the failure of the long pursuit of solutions through political means in India, there are signs that the chief impetus for such a reformulation may come from the increasingly confident and well-established diaspora communities now settled for over a generation in Britain, Canada, and the USA, totalling about one million, and even numerically significant in relation to the fifteen million Indian Sikhs.

The Sikh diasporas remain closely linked to the Punjab, through family ties, the rituals of the *gurdwara* and the great Sikh festivals (*gurpurbs*), and regular pilgrimages to the great shrines associated with the Gurus. But they are also directly exposed to their Western environments, and relatively free from the constraints felt within an increasingly Hindu-dominated India, encouraging the emergence of a new intellectual leadership, based within Western universities and using English rather than Punjabi as its prime medium of expression.

Several emerging trends may be signalled as pointers. A new critical attention is being given to sensitive topics, notably the study of the formation of the scripture, and the interpretation of key mythic episodes of Sikh history, such as the foundation of the *Khalsa*. There is also a revaluation of the importance of other traditions within Sikhism that were marginalized by the triumph of the reformed *Khalsa,* to whom the SGPC *Rehat Maryada* almost exclusively refers, neglecting the many who follow the teachings of Guru Nanak and his successors, but do not observe the full *Khalsa* discipline. And women's voices are starting to be articulated in a religious tradition that has been so powerfully dominated by the bearded male presence. These and other trends have yet to coalesce; but it seems certain that traditional authority will become subject to increasing challenges, as Sikhism – like all other religions – grapples with an ever-changing modern world.

CHRISTOPHER SHACKLE

QUESTIONS

1. Explain the role of Guru Nanak's example in Sikhism.

2. Why does Sikhism reject asceticism?

3. Why is the *Adi Granth* so revered?

4. Why does Sikhism reject the caste system?

5. How have Hinduism and Islam influenced Sikhism?

6. How do Sikhs believe they can overcome *chaurasi* (the cycle of death and rebirth)?

7. How far was the Tenth Guru responsible for shaping Sikhism?

8. Explain the importance of the *Khalsa* in Sikhism.

9. What factors are responsible for the tension between Sikhism and the Indian state in recent decades?

10. How important is the *Rehat Maryada* to the development of Sikhism in recent decades?

FURTHER READING

Brown, Kerry, *Sikh Art and Literature*. London: Routledge, 1999.

Fenech, Louis E., *Martyrdom in the Sikh Tradition: Playing the Game of Love*. Delhi: Oxford University Press, 2000.

McLeod, W. H., *Historical Dictionary of Sikhism*. Lanham, MD: Scarecrow Press, 1995.

McLeod, W. H., *Sikhism*. London: Penguin, 1997.

Nat, J. S., *The Sikhs of the Punjab*. Cambridge: Cambridge University Press, 2008.

O'Connell, Joseph T., Milton Israel, and Willard G. Oxtoby, eds., *Sikh History and Religion in the Twentieth Century*. Toronto: University of Toronto Centre for South Asian Studies, 1988.

Shackle, Christopher ed., *Sikh Religion, Culture and Ethnicity*. Richmond, Surrey: Curzon, 2001.

Singh, Patwant, *The Sikhs*. New York: Knopf, 2000.

GALLERY

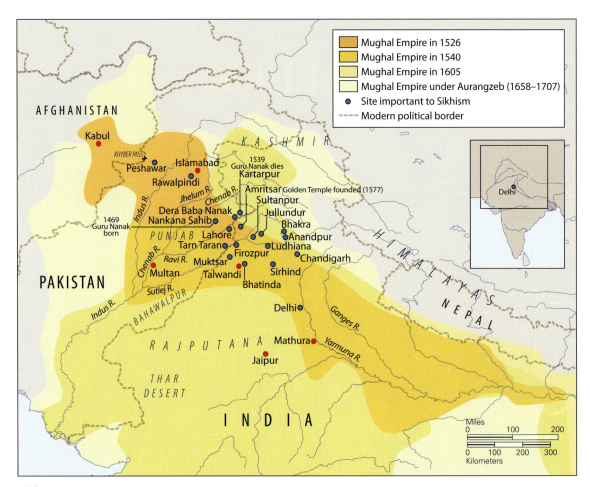

Sikh Origins

The map shows:

Legend:
- Mughal Empire in 1526
- Mughal Empire in 1540
- Mughal Empire in 1605
- Mughal Empire under Aurangzeb (1658–1707)
- Site important to Sikhism
- Modern political border

Labels on map:

AFGHANISTAN

Kabul

KHYBER PASS

Peshawar

Islamabad

1539
Guru Nanak dies
Kartarpur

KASHMIR

Rawalpindi

Jhelum R.

Chenab R.

Amritsar   Golden Temple founded (1577)

Sultanpur

Dera Baba Nanak

Jullundur

Indus R.

Nankana Sahib

1469
Guru Nanak
born

Bhakra

Lahore

Anandpur

PUNJAB

Chenab R.

Tarn Taran

Ludhiana

Ravi R.

Firozpur

Muktsar

Chandigarh

PAKISTAN

Multan

Talwandi

Sirhind

Bhatinda

HIMALAYAS

NEPAL

Sutlej R.

BAHAWALPUR

Delhi

Indus R.

Ganges R.

RAJPUTANA

Mathura

Yarmuna R.

Jaipur

THAR
DESERT

INDIA

Delhi

Miles
0   100   200

0   100   200   300
Kilometers

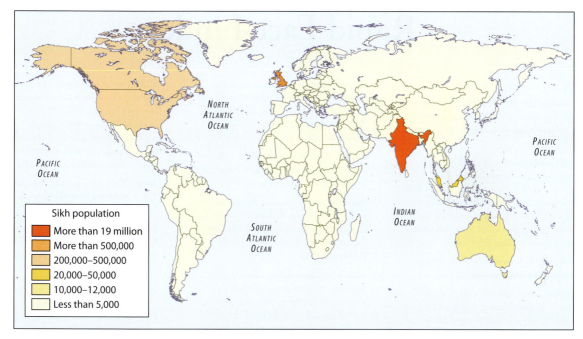

Sikhism Worldwide Today

Rapid Fact-Finder

A

Absolute, The Term for God or the divine often preferred by those who conceive of God predominantly in abstract or impersonal terms.

Adi Granth Sacred book of Sikhism. It is regarded as the eternal Guru for the Sikh community. It is the central focus of the Sikh home and of the Gurdwara. The tenth guru, Gobind Singh, said that after him the final and perpetual guru would be the Adi Granth, to be known as Guru Granth Sahib.

Afterlife Any form of conscious existence after the death of the body.

Ahimsa Indian virtue of non-violence. It usually applies to abstention from harming any living creature and hence to vegetarianism. The doctrine was developed in Jainism, Buddhism, and some Hindu sects. In Jain belief violence carries severe penalties of karma. Mahatma Gandhi applied the idea to the political struggles of the oppressed in his practice of non-violent non-cooperation.

Allah The Muslim name for God. Allah is one; there are no other gods. As pure, undivided spirit, Allah is the creator and sustainer of all that is known to human beings in the revelation of the divine will in the Qur'an. Throughout the Qur'an, Allah is declared to be 'the merciful' and 'the compassionate'.

All-India Muslim League Organization founded in 1906 CE to promote the interests and political aspirations of Indian Muslims.

Amritsar Site of the Golden Temple, the holiest shrine of the Sikh religion, completed by Arjan, the fifth Guru.

Ancestor veneration The practice in indigenous religions of making offerings to the spirits of the dead and expecting to communicate with them through dreams.

Animism A term formerly used to describe pre-literary religions. It was dropped because its meaning, 'spiritism', was felt to be misleading.

Archetypes Term invented by C. G. Jung to describe the concepts held in common by different people at different times and in different places. He believed that the concept of God was the archetype of the self and that it was the object of each individual to discover it.

Aristotle (384–322 BCE) Greek philosopher and scientist who taught on every branch of knowledge valued in his time.

Asceticism Austere practices designed to lead to the control of the body and the senses. These may include fasting and meditation, the renunciation of possessions, and the pursuit of solitude.

Ashram In Indian religion, a hermitage or monastery. It has come to denote a communal house for devotees of a guru. It functions as a centre for building up the commitment of believers and for transmitting the guru's message.

Atman Sanskrit word meaning soul or self. The Upanishads teach that *atman* is identical to brahman, i.e. the soul is one with the divine.

Austerity Ascetic practice in which one exercises self-restraint or denial, for example, the restriction of food during a fast.

Avatar ('one who descends') In popular Hinduism, Lord Vishnu appears on earth at intervals to assert ancient values and destroy illusion. Krishna is the most famous *avatar*. Some modern cults claim to worship a living *avatar*.

B

Benares/Varanasi/Kashi The most holy city of Hinduism, situated on the banks of the Ganges. It is a centre for the worship of Shiva and attracts a million pilgrims every year.

Bhagavan/Bhagwan Indian title meaning 'lord' or 'worshipful'. It is frequently used of Vishnu. It is also a title of honour used by devotees of holy men.

Bhajana An Indian song or hymn in praise of God usually sung communally at devotional gatherings and accompanied by musical instruments.

Bhakti Love of, or devotion to, God. It is one of the Hindu paths to union with God (*see* yoga). It is expressed in popular religion in which the worshipper develops a sense of personal relationship to God, responding to him as though to a father, mother, friend, lover, or child, and looking to him for grace.

Brahma The creator god of Hinduism. With Vishnu and Shiva, Brahma belongs to the Trimurti of classical Hindu thought.

Buddhism The religion which developed from the teaching of the Buddha and which spread from India into south-east Asia, later expanding into northern Asia, China and Japan.

C

Caste system The division of a society into groups reflecting and defining the division of labour. In Hinduism, caste is traditionally seen as the creation of Brahma, each caste emerging symbolically from different parts of his body. There are four chief groups (*varnas*): Brahmins, priests, come from Brahma's mouth; Kshatriyas, warriors, come from Brahma's arms; Vaishyas, commoners, come from Brahma's thighs; Sudras, servants, come from Brahma's feet. Groups of no definite caste were regarded as Untouchables and were banished from society.

Chakras According to Indian thought and many contemporary alternative spiritualities, there are seven (sometimes six) chakras (meaning 'wheels') or spiritual energy centres located in the human body. They are: at the top of the head; between the eyebrows; at the throat; at the heart; at the navel; at the genitals; and at the base of the spine, where kundalini, the serpent-energy, lies coiled. The chakras are sometimes called 'lotus centres'.

Chela In Indian religion, a disciple, student, or follower of a guru.

Civil religion Religion as a system of beliefs, symbols, and practices which legitimate the authority of a society's institutions and bind people together in the public sphere.

Conversion A moral or spiritual change of direction, or the adoption of religious beliefs not previously held.

Cosmology (1) The study of the nature of the cosmos. (2) In religion, cosmologies concern the relationship between the divine and the natural world. This relationship is usually described in myths or stories of how God or the gods had brought the world, humanity, and particular peoples into existence and how they continue to relate to them. Cosmologies form the frameworks within which reality is interpreted.

Creation The act of God by which the universe came into being. Hence also refers to the universe itself. In Hinduism it is believed that the universe has been outpoured from God and will contract into him at the end of the age.

Creation myth A story that explains the divine origins of a particular people, a place or the whole world. In some indigenous religions and ancient religions it is ritually re-enacted at the beginning of each year.

D

Dasara An Indian festival usually celebrated in October. Different parts of India celebrate the festival in different ways and focus on different deities. The celebrations vary from a day to nine days to a month. Those who celebrate it as '*Dussehra*' worship the goddess Durga or celebrate Rama's victory over Ravana.

Dharma In Hinduism, cosmic order, the law of existence, right conduct.

Diaspora The geographical spread of a people who share a common culture.

Dietary laws Rules about food and drink that are characteristic of a particular religion. Jainism bans all animal products.

Disciple Followers of a religious leader or teaching.

Divination The art of the diviner.

Diwali Festival of light celebrated by Hindus, Jains, and Sikhs. For Jains it is the beginning of a new ritual and commercial year and celebrates Mahavira's transcendence to moksha and the enlightenment of his disciple

Gautama. For Sikhs it is a commemoration of the release from prison of the sixth Guru and his return to the city of Amritsar.

Doctrine A religious teaching or belief which is taught and upheld within a particular religious community.

Dravidian Word describing the pre-Aryan civilization based in the Indus valley. It was overturned by Aryan invaders around 2000 BCE. Today Dravidian peoples inhabit southern India.

E

Esoteric Word meaning 'inner', suggesting something (e.g. a knowledge or a teaching) that is available only for the specially initiated and secret from outsiders and perhaps even from ordinary believers.

Exorcism Removal of sin or evil, particularly an evil spirit in possession of someone, by prayer or ritual action.

F

Faith Attitude of belief, in trust and commitment to a divine being or a religious teaching. It can also refer to the beliefs of a religion, 'the faith', which is passed on from teachers to believers.

Fasting Total or partial abstinence from food, undertaken as a religious discipline. It is also more generally used as a means of gaining clarity of vision and mystical insight.

Four stages of life Hindu outline of a man's ideal spiritual life. There are four stages (ashramas): student, the Hindu boy learns the scriptures in the house of his guru and lives a life of chastity; householder, he marries, has children and earns his living; retired life, when his family are grown up he gradually begins to withdraw from everyday life; renounced life, where he cuts all earthly ties and seeks liberation, often as a wandering beggar.

G

Ganesha Elephant-headed god much loved in popular Hinduism, especially in western India. He is the god of good beginnings and is a symbol for luck and wealth in business and daily life.

Ganges The holy river of India whose waters are sacred for all Hindus. It is thought to flow from the toe of Vishnu. Pilgrims wash away evil in its waters and the ashes of the dead are thrown into it.

Ghat ('holy place') In Hindu use, a word which can refer to a range of hills, a ritual bathing place, or a cremation ground.

Gobind Singh, Guru (1666–1708 CE) The tenth Guru of the Sikh community. He formalized the Sikh religion, requiring Sikhs to adopt a distinctive name and dress. He also shifted the focus of authority from the Gurus to the sacred scripture, the Adi Granth.

God (1) The creator and sustainer of the universe; the absolute being on whom all that is depends. (2) A being with divine power and attributes; a deity, a major Divinity.

Goddess (1) Female form of god. (2) The supreme being conceived as female as in some modern Pagan religious movements. Worshippers of the Goddess claim that they are continuing the ancient religion of the Mother Goddess who was a personification of nature.

Gurdwara Sikh temple and meeting place, consisting of a worship area which houses the Guru Granth Sahib, and a cooking and eating area, the *langar*, for the meal which ends Sikh worship.

Guru ('teacher') A spiritual teacher or guide who, in Indian religion, awakens a disciple to a realization of his or her own divine nature. In Sikh religion it refers to the ten teachers, from Guru Nanak to Guru Gobindh Singh, who ruled the community.

Guru Granth Sahib *see* **Adi Granth**.

H

Hanuman Monkey-god of popular Hinduism. In the Ramayana he led a monkey army against a host of demons. He can fly and cover huge distances at great speed.

Heaven The realm of God or of the gods.

Hindu Word used by Arabs to describe people living beyond the Indus Valley. Today it refers generally to people practising Indian religion who are neither Muslim, Sikh, Parsi, nor Jain, and also to their religion, Hinduism.

Hinduism A term coined by Europeans for a religious tradition and social system that emerged in India. It has no founder, no set creed, no prophets, and no single institutional structure. It is actually an umbrella term for an enormous range of beliefs and practices, from the worship of local village deities to the thought of a great philosopher such as Shankara. There are, however, some common beliefs which are basic to most strands of Hinduism. There is an emphasis on dharma (the right way of living) rather than assent to particular doctrines. Also found throughout Hinduism is the notion of moksha, or release from the eternal cycle of birth, death, and rebirth (samsara) to which one is bound by karma. Linked to this set of beliefs is the social stratification known as the caste system. The three chief Hindu deities are Brahma, Vishnu, and Shiva, who together form a triad known as the Trimurti. Numerous other deities are worshipped, but all are aspects of the universal spirit, Brahman. Hindus' concepts of God are complex and largely depends upon the Indian traditions and philosophy followed.

Humanism Way of life based on the belief that what is good for human beings is the highest good.

Hymn A sacred song sung in the context of communal worship; a psalm of communal praise. Hymns are particularly important in Christian and Sikh worship and in the gatherings of the Hindu bhakti cults.

I

Icon A likeness of a divine figure or saint painted on wood or inland in mosaic and used in public or private devotion.

Incense Sweet-smelling smoke used in worship, made by burning certain aromatic substances.

Indigenous religions The preferred term for religions which are sometimes referred to as 'primal', 'tribal', 'traditional', 'primitive', and 'non-/pre-literate' religions. That said, indigenous religions are often developments of the traditional religions of tribal and aboriginal cultures. The problem with the earlier terminology was that it suggested simple, undeveloped, non-progressive, and archaic belief systems. Contemporary indigenous religions include Native American religion and Australian Aboriginal religion.

Initiation Ceremony marking coming of age, or entry into adult membership of a community. It is also used of the secret ceremonies surrounding membership of the mystery religions.

J

Jain ('one who has conquered') A follower of the religion known as Jainism.

Jainism Religion of India that derives its name from Jina (conqueror). This term (and the related term Tirthankara) is used of a religious teacher who is believed to have attained enlightenment and omniscience. The most recent Jina was Mahavira, who is regarded as the founder of Jainism. Early in its history Jainism separated into two main sects: Digambara Jainism and Shvetambara Jainism. (*See also* Digambara; Jina, Jiva; Mahavira; Parsva; Shvetambara.)

Jinas Also called *'Tirthankaras'* ('ford-makers'), *Jinas* ('conquerors') are Jain religious teachers who have attained enlightenment and omniscience by conquering samsara (the continuous cycle of birth, death, and rebirth to which those with karma are bound).

Jiva A soul or 'life monad' according to Jain belief. Jivas are infinite and omniscient but in this world Karma weighs them down into a material existence. Jivas are liberated by acquiring omniscience, and this makes them float up to the summit of the universe.

Judgment The divine assessment of individuals and the settling of their destinies, a notion found in many religions.

Jung, C. G. (Carl Gustav) (1875–1961 CE) Swiss psychiatrist who invented the theory of archetypes. He investigated the significance of myths, symbols, and dreams, and found in them evidence for a 'collective unconscious' which was at the root of religion.

K

Kabir (c. 1440–1518) Indian poet and hymn writer who influenced the development of early Sikhism. He attempted a synthesis of Islam and Hinduism, rejecting the caste system and circumcision, but teaching the love of God, rebirth, and liberation.

Karma Sanskrit word for work or action. In Indian belief every action has inevitable consequences which attach themselves to the doer requiring reward or punishment. Karma is thus the moral law of cause and effect. It explains the inequalities of life as the consequences of actions in previous lives. The notion of karma probably developed among the Dravidian people of India.

Kashi *see* **Benares**.

Khalsa Originally the militant community of Sikhs organized by Guru Gobind Singh in 1699 CE. Now it is the society of fully committed adult members of the Sikh community. Membership is signified by the 'Five Ks': uncut hair, a comb worn in the hair, a small dagger, shorts, and an iron or steel bracelet.

Krishna The eighth incarnation of Vishnu according to Hindu tradition. His name means 'black'. Though of noble birth, he was brought up as a cowherd. Eventually he obtained his inheritance and ruled in justice. He was also a great lover: the Mahabharata describes his romances with the cow-girls which are seen as a type of God's love for the soul (1). He is also the main character in the Bhagavad Gita, where he appears disguised as the charioteer of Prince Arjuna.

L

Laity (from Greek laos, 'people') The non-ordained members of a religious community, or those with no specialist religious function.

Lakshmi Lord Vishnu's consort. She appears in the *Rig Veda* (*see* Vedas) as good fortune. In the Ramayana she rises out of the sea holding a lotus. She is involved in Vishnu's descents to earth as an avatar. Some associate her with Sita and Radha, the consorts of Rama and Krishna.

Libation The ritual outpouring of drink as an offering to divinities or ancestor spirits.

M

Magic The manipulation of natural or supernatural forced by spells and rituals for good or harmful ends.

Mahabharata One of the two great epics of the Hindu scriptures compiled by the third or second century BCE. Ascribed to the sage Vyasa, it tells of the war between two families, the Kauravas and the Pandus. The divine hero of the epic is the avatar Krishna.

Mahavira Great Jain teacher who traditionally lived 599–527 BCE, though this is disputed. He abolished the distinctions of the caste system and tried to spread his teaching among the Brahmins. He starved himself to death at the age of seventy-two, having spent his last years totally naked.

Mantra A symbolic sound causing an internal vibration which helps to concentrate the mind and aids self-realization, e.g. the repeated syllable 'om'. In Hinduism the term originally referred to a few sacred verses from the Vedas. It came to be thought that they possessed spiritual power, and that repetition of them was a help to liberation. A mantra is sometimes given by a spiritual teacher to a disciple as an initiation.

Meditation Deep and continuous reflection, practised in many religions with a variety of aims, e.g. to attain self-realization or, in theistic religions, to attain union with the divine will.

Medium One who is possessed by the spirit of a dead person or a divinity and, losing his or her individual identity, becomes the mouthpiece for the other's utterance.

Miracle An event which appears to defy rational explanation and is attributed to divine intervention.

Mission The outreach of a religion to the unconverted. Whereas understandings of mission vary from faith to faith, the various aims of mission usually include spiritual conversion. However, mission is often conceived more holistically and concerns, not just spiritual conversion, but the transformation of all areas of life. It addresses injustice, suffering, poverty, racism, sexism, and all forms of oppression.

Mohammed *see* **Muhammad**.

Moksha Sanskrit word meaning liberation from the cycle of birth, death, and rebirth. Permanent spiritual perfection experienced by an enlightened soul after the physical body has died. No further incarnations will be endured.

Monk A member of a male religious community living under vows which usually include poverty, chastity, and the wearing of a distinctive form of dress. Monastic orders are found in Christianity, Buddhism, Hinduism, and Jainism.

Monotheism The belief that there is one supreme God who contains all the attributes and characteristics of divinity.

Muhammad (c. 570–632 CE) Prophet and apostle of Islam, the final messenger of God whose message, the Qur'an, sums up and completes the previous revelations to the Jews and Christians. Muhammad saw the expansion of Islam in terms of military conquest and political organization and he was outstandingly successful as a commander and ruler in Medina and later Mecca.

Muslim 'One who submits' to the will of God, a follower of Islam.

Mystic One who seeks direct personal experience of the divine and may use prayer, meditation or various ascetic practices to concentrate the attention.

Myth A sacred story which originates and circulates within a particular community. Some aetiological myths explain puzzling physical phenomena or customs, institutions and practices whose origin in the community would otherwise be mysterious.

N

Nanak, Guru (1469–1539 CE) Indian religious teacher and founder of the Sikh religion. He intended to reconcile Hindus and Muslims and travelled widely preaching a monotheistic faith (*see* monotheism) which was influenced by bhakti and Sufism. He appointed a successor to continue his teachings.

Nature spirits Spirits of trees, hills, rivers, plants, and animals which are acknowledged with prayers and offerings in most indigenous religions.

Nibbana Pali word for nirvana.

Nun A member of a religious community of women, as found in Christianity, Buddhism, hinduism, and Jainism. Nuns live under vows usually including poverty, and chastity and often the wearing of a distinctive form of dress.

O

Occult Teachings, arts, and practices that are concerned with what is hidden and mysterious, as with witchcraft, alchemy, and divination.

Omnipotence All-powerful.

Omniscience All-knowing. Simultaneous knowledge of all things.

P

Pagan/Paganism The word 'pagan' (derived from the Latin term *pagus*, which literally means 'from the countryside' or 'rural') was first used in a general religious sense by the early Christians to describe the non-Christian gentile religions. It is now generally used to refer to a broad range of nature-venerating religious traditions.

Palaeolithic period ('Old Stone Age') The prehistoric age covering from around 2.6 million years ago to c. 10,000 BCE.

Pantheism The belief that all reality is in essence divine.

Parsva Important figure in Jainism. Born a prince around 850 BCE he renounced his throne and became an ascetic, finally gaining omniscience. He is considered to be the twenty-third Jina.

Philosophy of religion The branch of philosophy which investigates religious experience considering its origin, context, and value.

Pilgrimage A journey to a holy place, undertaken as a commemoration of a past event, as a celebration, or as an act of penance. The goal might be a natural feature such as a sacred river or mountain, or the location of a miracle, revelation, or theophany, or the tomb of a hero or saint.

Plato (c. 427–347 BCE) Greek philosopher and pupil of Socrates. He taught the theory of Forms or Ideas, which are eternal prototypes of the phenomena encountered in ordinary experience. Above all is the Form of the Good, which gives unity and value to all the forms. Plato also taught the immortality of the soul.

Polytheism The belief in and worship of a variety of gods, who rule over various aspects of the world and life.

Prayer The offering of worship, requests, confessions, or other communication to God or gods publicly or privately, with or without words; often a religious obligation.

Prehistoric religion Religions dating from the period before the development of writing.

Priest One authorized to perform priestly functions including mediation between God or gods and humanity, the offerings of sacrifice and the performance of ritual in many religions.

Psalm A sacred song or poem.

Puja ('reverence') Refers to temple and domestic worship in Buddhism and Hinduism, and to the keeping of rites and ceremonies prescribed by the Brahmins (*see* caste system).

Puranas A vast corpus of sacred writings (c. 350–950 CE), which include mythologies of Hindu deities and avatars of Vishnu, the origins of the cosmos, and of humanity, pilgrimage, ritual, law codes, caste obligations, and so on. There are eighteen principal Puranas, each exalting a member of the *Trimurti* (Brahma, Vishnu, Shiva). They are very important in popular Hinduism, Jainism, and Buddhism, the most popular being the *Bhagavata Purana*, which deals with Krishna's early life and encourages devotion to him (bhakti).

R

Rama The seventh incarnation of Vishnu according to Hindu tradition. His exploits in love and war are described in the Ramayana. He is the epitome of righteousness and moral virtue.

Ramayana One of the two great epics of the Hindu scriptures compiled in the second or first century BCE. Ascribe to the sage Valmiki, it tells of the life of the avatar Rama.

Religion (from Latin religare, 'to tie something tightly') A system of belief and worship, held by a community who may express its religion through shared myths, doctrines, ethical teachings, rituals, or the remembrance of special experiences.

Renunciation Giving up ownership of material possessions. In some religions, such as Buddhism, renunciation extends to psychological detachment from material possessions, including one's own body.

Rites of passage Religious ceremonies which mark the transition from one state of life to another. In many religions these transitional periods are felt to be dangerous and to require spiritual protection. Examples include birth rites, initiation rites, marriage rites, and funeral rites.

Ritual Religious ceremonial performed according to a set pattern of words, movements, and symbolic actions. Rituals may involve the dramatic re-enactment of ancient myths featuring gods and heroes, performed to ensure the welfare of the community.

S

Sacred Thread ceremony Initiation ceremony performed on Hindu and Buddhist boys. A sacred thread is placed around the neck indicating that the boy is one of the twice-born and has entered the first stage of life.

Sacrifice The ritual offering of animal or vegetable life to establish communion between humans and a god or gods.

Salvation In Eastern religions, release from the changing material world to identification with the absolute.

Samsara ('stream of existence') Sanskrit word which refers to the cycle of birth and death followed by rebirth as applied both to individuals and to the universe itself.

Sanctuary A place consecrated to a god, a holy place, a place of divine refuge and protection. Also, the holiest part of a sacred place or building.

Sannyasi ('one who renounces') The last of the Hindu Four Stages of Life.

Sanskrit The language of the Aryan peoples and of the Hindu scriptures. It is an Indo-European language related to Latin, Greek, and Persian.

Sarasvati In Hinduism, the goddess of truth and consort of Brahma, the Creator.

Satguru (1) In Sikhism, God, the true and eternal Guru. (2) In popular Hinduism a term for a revered teacher such as Sai Baba.

Scripture Writings which are believed to be divinely inspired or especially authoritative within a particular religious community.

Sect A group, usually religious (but it can be political), which has separated itself from an established tradition, claiming to teach and practise a truer form of the faith from which it has separated itself. It is, as such, often highly critical of the wider tradition which it has left.

Shiva One of the great gods of Hindu devotion. He is a god of contrasts, presiding over creation and destruction, fertility and asceticism, good, and evil. He is the original Lord of the Dance who dances out the creation of the universe. As god of ascetics he is portrayed as a great *yogi*, smeared with ashes, holding the world in being through meditation. His symbol is a phallus-shaped pillar denoting procreation.

Shvetambara ('white-clad') Member of a major Jain sect who rejected the Digambara stress on the virtues of nudity. They are numerous in the north of India.

Sikh ('disciple') Follower of the Sikh religion which developed in the fifteenth century CE in northern India as a synthesis of Islam and Hinduism. (*See also* Adi Granth; Gobindh Singh; Gurdwara; Kabir; Khalsa; Nanak; Singh.)

Sin An action which breaks a divine law.

Singh Surname used by Sikhs when they become a member of the khalsa. It means 'lion' and expresses the militant stance which Guru Gobindh Singh impressed upon the Sikh community.

Sorcerer A practitioner of harmful magic. In indigenous religions sorcerers are sometimes believed to be able to kill others through magic.

Soteriology Teaching about salvation.

Soul (1) The immortal element of an individual man or woman which survives the death of the body in most religious teachings. (2) A human being when regarded as a spiritual being.

Spiritualism Any religious system or practice which has the object of establishing communication with the dead.

Swami General term for a Hindu holy man or member of a religious order.

Swaminarayan (1781–1830 CE) Gujarati preacher and founder of a popular sect which attracted Sikh and Hindu followers.

Syncretism The growing together of two or more religions making a new development in religion which contains some of the beliefs and practices of both.

T

Tao ('way') In Taoism, the underlying principle of reality.

Taoism Chinese philosophy outlined in the Tao Te Ching. Its aim is to achieve harmony with all that is by pursuing inaction and effortlessness. Taoism gradually evolved an elaborate mythological system and incorporated notions of spirit possession, alchemy, and divination. (*See also* Jade Emperor; Lao-tzu.)

Temple Building designed for worship of God or gods, usually containing a sanctuary or holy place where sacrifice may be offered.

Ten Gurus In Sikhism Guru Nanak and his nine successors who are seen as sharing the same essential insights into the nature of God.

Theism The belief in one supreme God who is both transcendent and involved in the workings of the universe.

Theology A systematic formulation of belief made by or on behalf of a particular individual or church or other body of believers.

W

Worship Reverence or homage to God or a god which may involve prayer, sacrifice, rituals, singing, dancing, or chanting.

Y

Yogi Indian holy man who has reached enlightenment through yogic practices (*see* yoga). (*See also* Transcendental Meditation.)

Index

Numbers in **bold type** indicate pages with illustrations.
The Rapid Fact-Finder is not indexed.

Picture Acknowledgments

Dreamstime pp. 18, 31, 40, 43, 46, 55, 64, 72, 76, 79, 103, 108, 115

Illustrated London News pp. 15, 34

Photodisc p. 27

Tim Dowley Associates pp. 37, 89, 99, 106